Brandsplaining

'Filled with fascinating and funny insights, *Brandsplaining* is not just about marketing but also about how gender identities can be (and are) shaped and misshaped, branded and rebranded. If you think we've moved on from "Good Girl" to "Go Girl", think again! This is great food for thought in any debates about the path to gender irrelevance – or even gender neutrality' Professor Gina Rippon, author of *The Gendered Brain*

'What an important piece of research, and what an interesting read! This book has the power to change the way that people see everything' Sophie Devonshire, CEO of The Marketing Society

'A brilliant book – witty and wise. A fast-track primer to gender bilingual marketing: the skill of being able to connect with 100 per cent of your potential market and avoid the lazy, systemic default of outdated and ineffective brandsplaining' Avivah Wittenberg-Cox, CEO of 20-first

'An outrageously important book. Erudite, funny, and deeply engaging – with no condescension or bullshit – *Brandsplaining* sets out why the male monologue continues to monopolize, and what to do about it' Dr Aarathi Prasad, author of *Like a Virgin*

'On our way to dethroning patriarchy's hold on capitalism, books like this are critical. It's high time we expose and remedy the pseudo-feminist marketing malarkey holding women back under the guise of empowerment. *Brandsplaining* is here to help us do just that' Amanda Montell, author of *Wordslut*

Jane Cunningham and Philippa Roberts both began their careers working in advertising and communications agencies. As they rose through the ranks to become part of the leadership teams at DDB and at Ogilvy, they repeatedly noticed how female customers were perceived in ways that were at best inaccurate and at worst diminishing and dismissive.

After over ten years of attempting to right the wrong from the inside, they decided enough was enough, and left to set up their own research company, PLH, with the specific intention of helping the marketing world better understand female audiences.

In the years that have followed, they have spent almost every week enjoyably conducting research on behalf of a wide range of clients, exploring what women feel about themselves, and the businesses and brands that profess to serve them.

They have been described as 'the pioneers of marketing to women' and *The Times* has written of their work: 'Jane Cunningham and Philippa Roberts argued that marketing departments need to work much harder at understanding women's motivations and decision-making systems. They won the argument. This is a crude generalization, but not one, I think, with which most will disagree. Creative briefs have radically changed to favour emotional intelligence and impact over rational, white-coated persuasion.'

They are also the authors of two books on marketing to women, and have regularly appeared in the media discussing the subject.

Brandsplaining

*Why Marketing is Still Sexist and
How to Fix It*

JANE CUNNINGHAM AND
PHILIPPA ROBERTS

BUSINESS

PENGUIN BUSINESS

UK | USA | Canada | Ireland | Australia
India | New Zealand | South Africa

Penguin Business is part of the Penguin Random House group of companies
whose addresses can be found at global.penguinrandomhouse.com.

First published 2021
001

Copyright © Jane Cunningham and Philippa Roberts, 2021

The moral right of the authors has been asserted

Set in 12/14.75 pt Dante MT Std
Typeset by Jouve (UK), Milton Keynes
Printed and bound in Great Britain by Clays Ltd, Elcograf S.p.A.

The authorized representative in the EEA is Penguin Random House Ireland,
Morrison Chambers, 32 Nassau Street, Dublin D02 YH68

A CIP catalogue record for this book is available from the British Library

ISBN: 978-0-241-45600-2

Follow us on LinkedIn: https://www.linkedin.com/company/penguin-connect/

To our research subjects who went to great lengths to come to our sessions and still arrived in good spirits:

Thank you for swapping your shift and owing your friend a favour; for begging your always obliging mother-in-law to mind your kids yet again; for waiting at the bus stop when it was raining; for sticking your jeans in the dryer so you didn't have to wear your leggings (not that we would have cared); for filling the slow cooker so you could stay 'til the end. Thank you for all that stuff that you did, and for telling us everything we needed to know.

Contents

Contents

Preface: On Mansplaining

Chances are you already know the term 'mansplaining', and, better still, that you already know Rebecca Solnit's famous and influential essay 'Men Explain Things to Me', from which the term was derived. But, for those of you who don't (and, if you haven't read it, can we urge you to look it up: it is one of those pieces that takes ten minutes to read but genuinely changes the way you see the world for ever), let's do a quick piece of our own explaining.

Rebecca Solnit is a distinguished academic who, in 2003, had recently published her seventh book – *River of Shadows: Eadweard Muybridge and the Technological Wild West* (don't worry, we'd never heard of him either and you don't need to know who he was in order to get the story).

In 'Men Explain Things to Me' she describes how, just after her book had come out, she and a friend were invited to a drinks party hosted by an older man. On being informed by Solnit that she had just published a book on Muybridge, he proceeded to tell her the news that 'a very important' book on Muybridge had also recently come out. Solnit's friend tried tactfully to interrupt his flow to say that the book he was describing was, in fact, written by the person he was talking to, but the man – 'with that smug look I know so well in a man holding forth, eyes fixed on the fuzzy far horizon of his own authority' – just continued on his way, explaining to Solnit her own book and its contents.

Only after three or four more interruptions did the penny finally drop (though apparently no apology was forthcoming).

'I like incidents of that sort,' writes Solnit, 'when forces that are usually so sneaky and hard to point out slither out of the grass and are as obvious as say an anaconda that's eaten a cow or an elephant turd on the carpet.'

From this incident and the brilliant essay on assumed male authority that it precipitated, the term 'mansplaining' was born. And it spread, in the dazzling way that the internet now allows these things to catch fire, because it put a label on something that women have known, and been on the receiving end of, for centuries: that tendency, in certain men, to talk to women as if they are 'an empty vessel to be filled with their wisdom and knowledge'.

The term is brilliant because it suddenly gives a name to one of those hidden-in-the-woodwork biases that work to allocate women a secondary place in the conversation. It pulls into the light a discourse where the speaker assumes he is the greater authority on the subject and so can talk down to the listener, treating her as someone who can be told. And where the listener, as a result of the assumed authority, begins to feel that maybe she does know less and should perhaps be a mere recipient rather than an equal participant. (Rebecca Solnit rather sadly describes how, despite her incredible achievements and her seven published books, 'so caught up was I in my assigned role as ingénue that I was perfectly willing to entertain the possibility that another book on the same subject had come out simultaneously and I'd somehow missed it'.)

Most revealingly, perhaps, 'mansplaining' gives a term to the unbalanced relationship where the speaker is so bound by his own bias that he cannot hear or accommodate any alternative, ploughing on with his own categorical but erroneous assumptions, telling the audience what to think and how to be, even after being presented with compelling evidence to the contrary.

In fact, so insightful is the term that we have shamelessly bastardized it for our own purposes. The title of this book, *Brandsplaining*, sums up in a single word the heart of the dominant problem that currently exists between brands and the female audiences they profess to serve. And that problem is this: that despite women representing the most valuable target audience on earth, and despite the immense progress and achievements of women throughout the world on both a micro and macro level, and despite the fact that the last decade has seen an upending of traditional notions of gender and male–female relationships – despite all of this, the majority of brands still speak to women from a male perspective, explaining to them what they are and telling them what they can be.

This book is about unpacking why that happens, how the male perspective comes to dominate, the unequal and unlistening relationship that results and the impacts that it has both on women and on brands. It is about pulling into the light the (to borrow yet more of Rebecca Solnit's words) 'sneaky and hard to point out' behaviours and unconscious biases that can shape the conversation between brands and their female audiences. And it's then – on the basis of all that understanding – about showing and suggesting what can be done to eliminate and replace those biases in order to create brands and communications that forge more constructive relationships with female audiences.

Introduction: Why Marketing Really Is Still Sexist

Funnily enough, the catalyst for this book was a mansplaining moment of our own.

It happened a few years ago at one of those women's-network conferences that businesses run to support their female employees. You may well have been to one, and you undoubtedly know how they come about: 'Let's get some women in to talk to some other women about some things to do with women. We could call it #AdvanceHer. Lynda from Human Capital Management would love to take it all on. Provided it's in addition to her day job. I'd be happy to act as sponsor.'

We had been invited to the conference to speak about our specialism – marketing to women. We run a research business that specializes in the female audience. We set the business up just over fifteen years ago after both having worked in senior jobs in advertising. During our time in the advertising industry we'd developed an increasing sense that women were under-served and under-understood as an audience, so we left our jobs and set up shop as Europe's first research consultants specializing in understanding women. The opportunity, as we saw it, was to provide businesses and their agencies with an appreciation of what the modern female consumer was really like. Who was she? What was she thinking and feeling and wanting and needing? How was she different by age, geography, affluence, and socio-demographic group and what were those differences? What did she feel about herself and her life – and her hopes? What did she really need and value in the categories and the brands that she bought?

So, there we were, at this event, ready to give a perspective on marketing to women based on over a decade spent researching the subject with women themselves. At the awkward-milling-around-drinking-stale-filter-coffee stage of the proceedings, one of the few men attending the conference introduced himself and we heard from him the usual prosaic 'So what brings you here?' preamble that often gets cast more glamorously as 'networking'.

We explained that we ran a research company that specialized in marketing to women, and were at the event to contribute a from-the-research perspective on how women were changing. In particular, we were going to make the argument that marketing was failing to understand and reflect those changes, and was in many, usually unconscious, ways still casting women as secondary.

At this point, it would be terribly convenient to report that – like Rebecca Solnit's Very Important Man – our version proceeded to clear his throat and hold forth on the subject of women, how he believed they were changing, how he had observed that marketing was failing to understand and reflect those changes, and had we ourselves noticed that marketing was, in many usually unconscious ways, still talking to women in ways that cast them as secondary?

Annoyingly, it didn't happen quite as neatly or, in fact, as nicely as that: instead our man appeared very courteous, nodded and hmmm-ed earnestly . . . and then proceeded to argue entirely against our proposition.

'I think you're totally wrong,' he said. 'It's ridiculous. I don't think there's any problem with marketing to women now. Ten years ago, yes: maybe, things were a bit sexist and out-of-date. But that's not the case now. If anything, the opposite is true. Look at Dove. Look at Nike. Look at Like A Girl. Look at . . .'

The man then proceeded – in the manner of the most fervent barrister getting into his 'if it may please the court' stride – to lay out his case for why marketing to women was now a non-problem. On and on he went, citing his evidence, telling us why we were wrong to think there was still an issue, why any problem there was had been fixed, and why, moreover, 'It's all moved on. It's not about that now. Sustainability is where it's at.'

Before he had time to complete his takedown with an 'I rest my case' flourish – or one of us had the opportunity to adopt the Rebecca Solnit's Friend role and 'splain back to him the basis of our argument, and the fact that we'd actually spent 4,000 hours over fifteen years researching the very subject, or that we'd published two books that examined the issues in detail – the conference resumed and we were obliged to return to proceedings while our Very Important Man – let's call him Steve – rode off confidently on his high horse.

And despite having the spring slightly taken out of our step just moments before we were due to speak, Steve's remarks weren't really that remarkable. In fact, it's a view that we hear expressed frequently – and very often breezily – in the marketing and advertising communities: 'Marketing to women? Oh, that. No, that's not really a thing any more; admittedly it did used to be sexist, but it's all been sorted out now . . . Basically, move along ladies; nothing to see here; we've bigger fish to fry now.'

What is truly remarkable about this confident and very common assertion, however, is this: it's one hundred per cent wrong. And, to move the debate away from the subjective to the objective, we do actually know this for a fact. Over the fifteen years that we've spent researching brands and communications with female consumers, we've seen and heard again and again how those brands and those communications fail to understand women. And, over those years, we've conducted numerous situation, competitor and content analyses for clients across almost all categories – from the historically male sectors of politics, automotive, financial services, technology and utilities through to the classically 'feminine' spaces of beauty, fashion, babycare and sanitary products. We've researched women as old as ninety-four and girls as young as four; we've worked for high-end luxury brands and cut-price retailers; we've conducted projects in North America, Latin America, Europe and Asia-Pacific; we've researched through social and political shifts, upturns and recessions and, more recently, a global pandemic, exploring how women see the world, if and how their priorities are changing, and whether and how what they value has changed as the way we live is reappraised and reset.

And we have discovered themes that are strong and consistent across all these different contexts: while the above-the-surface, plain old sexism may be on the wane, beneath the surface a set of pronounced biases and assumptions continue to shape the way brands view their female audiences. Moreover, these biases reflect sexism at its most deep-rooted: not the obvious, plain-as-the-nose-on-your-face sexual objectification sort, but the hard-wired gendered views that unconsciously determine a world where women are cast as secondary.

So, for Steve and anyone who shares a Steve-like view of the situation, or, indeed, for anyone who recognizes the less widespread but more accurate view that there's still a problem, and still a long way to go to solve it, this book is for you. Perhaps a more fitting dedication would have been: 'To Steve. Without whom this book would never have been written (and without whom, it has to be said, it would not actually be necessary).'

But this book will also, we hope, be of use to those of you who aren't hanging out drinking coffee at conferences about marketing to women. If you're a parent, it will point out some of the reductive ways in which girls are presented in and marketed to by media; if you're a young woman it will reveal some of the ways in which your views of yourself are being shaped by the media around you – and so encourage you to see those presentations for the manipulations that they are; if you're a woman feeling the pressure to have it all and be it all, it will show you how much of that pressure is, in fact, artificial and, in more ways than one, man-made; if you're an older woman who feels invisible, it will tell you why you're made to feel like that – and why, moreover, it's ridiculous; if you're a female customer, buying from a company that claims, in any way, to 'serve' you, we want to give you a different perspective on how well they are actually doing that job. And if you're a man: we hope to help you see what we see.

In the first part of the book – 'How We Got Here' – we're going to take you on a brief tour of the history of marketing to women right up to the first decade of the twenty-first century. We will explore some of the hard-wired programming of marketing: the embedded and inbuilt factory settings that continue, usually unconsciously, to exert an influence on the way markets get segmented, audiences get viewed, brands get positioned and creative work gets generated.

Over the past fifteen years, there have been huge changes in how women see the world and how the world sees women. Around the globe we have seen some big advances in educational attainment, workforce participation, the ability to control fertility, anti-discrimination legislation and policies promoting work and family life balance. And we've also seen, and are seeing, some backlash and backsliding. So in Part Two – Where We Are Now – we're going to look at how marketing to women has responded to those changes – in particular, the era of what has been called (apologies, awful words, not ours) 'fempowerment' and 'femvertising'. We'll examine the to and fro of all those changes, and explore the areas where progress has been made, and where, sadly, it has not.

And then, in the third and final part of the book, we're going to look at where marketing to women needs to go next. As the Coronavirus pandemic continues to impact on consumer markets, behaviours and priorities, the need and opportunity for re-evaluation has never been more relevant or more urgent. While no one yet knows exactly what the emerging economy and new consumer priorities will look like, the history of major crises and their impacts does tell us this: major shocks to the system are invariably turning points for society.

Marketing to women has, for too long, lagged behind the way women are, and the new era offers an opportunity to reset and realign according to that reality. So in the final part of the book, we are going to look at the possibilities that emerge when the assumptions and biases of the past are removed. We will show how brands can reverse the 'brandsplaining' relationship, by seeing women as what they really are and want to be. We will propose ten simple principles to follow to overcome bias and enable that change to happen.

Our intention is that 'brandsplaining', in any of its forms, becomes visible and easy to identify, and feels so evidently inappropriate that it can be left in the past where it first began and where it now belongs. And that, finally, marketing to women can move on as fast as the audience it is making efforts to attract.

PART ONE

How We Got Here

The Origins of Brandsplaining

To begin right at the beginning, we need to go back to the twentieth century to look at how companies traditionally went about the business of marketing to women, and the assumptions upon which those approaches were based. We're starting here not because we want to rake over old coals or expose past misdemeanours but to examine and understand the original settings upon which marketing to women is based. These base settings continue to exert a profound, but often unconscious, influence on how marketing to women is conceived and conducted today. The settings are – to use Rebecca Solnit's words – the basis of the 'sneaky and hard to point out' forces that shape the way businesses approach the female audience: they are hard-wired into the way that categories are organized; they are embedded in the way in which women are seen and understood; and they are there, in the fine-grain of the development process, silently shaping everything from purpose to propositions through to presentation and production.

So, it is precisely in order to move forward that we need to go back: to understand how the relationships between men and women were seen and shaped in the past, and the foundational 'rules' of marketing to women that came about as a result.

And, in that spirit of beginning with base settings, let's begin with the basest setting of them all: modern-day sexism.

The foundations of modern sexism

When you ask someone to describe sexism and how it presents today, they'll almost invariably give you an answer that contains some sort of discriminatory behaviour against women: the builder shouting something lewd from the scaffolding; the older man saying something to the younger woman that she finds creepy but he thinks is charming; some sort of workplace incident that's a variation on that 'That's an excellent suggestion, Miss Triggs. Perhaps one of the men here would like to make it' cartoon.

But the truth of it is that modern-day sexism is a much more sneaky and surreptitious beast than the plain, out-there-for-all-to-see manifestations that are now, thankfully, on the wane. Where once it existed as an overt and obvious and pretty much deliberate piece of structural societal organization, the course of the twentieth century has seen sexism morph into something that largely operates below the surface: an 'invisible hand' that works in a stealthy and usually unseen way, silently influencing how things get done and the way things get seen.

The reality – and this is what is often misunderstood or overlooked – is that sexism is, in fact, a totalizing framework for seeing and thinking about women, what they are and what they can do. Like other -isms – communism, capitalism, Catholicism – it has a powerful internal logic which is tight, self-reflexive and resistant to challenge once it has taken root. Unlike other -isms, however, sexism traverses all economic models, most religions and almost all cultures. It is an all-pervasive system of power relations that silently influences the way that things get organized, and shapes the way we all – men, women, young, old, black, white, size 0, size 16 – see ourselves and the world around us.

And precisely because it is one of these invisible-hand forces, to understand sexism you need to unearth it, pull it out from its hiding place and examine it in the cold light of reality. So, at this point, we'll need to do a bit of 'splaining of our own, and lay out for you the essential tenets of sexism. Stand by as we treat you as 'an empty vessel to be filled with [our] wisdom and knowledge'.

The foundations of sexism begin with the starting point that men hold the positions of power and privilege in a society. There's some debate about how and where this situation arose, and for how long this has been the case, but it doesn't matter for the purposes of understanding. The point is that, since at least 4000 BCE, men have held the main positions of power.

At this stage of the argument, one of you will probably be putting up your hand and saying (slightly dismissively – is that you at the back again, Steve?) 'Well that might very well have been the case on the plains of the savannah or in ancient Mesopotamia or wherever, but things have changed a bit since then . . . women have lots of power now, look at our board, for example; we have three wonderful women . . .' But this time we're going to cut you straight off and answer right back: whatever the progress and power of women in developed societies (and we'll be looking at that in the other two parts of the book) the truth of it is this – in virtually every economy, and in virtually every walk of life, it is still mostly men who are mostly in charge for most of the time.

Now, under this construct women are necessarily cast into a less powerful secondary position where they are dependent on men's favour and support. This means that they have to behave in a way that is pleasing to men – being or presenting a version of themselves that men will find attractive, or helpful, or agreeable, or useful, and that won't, whatever it does, disrupt or threaten their status and power.

And it is from these unequal power relations that modern-day sexism comes: an endemic, hard-wired system of power relations where men are cast as primary and where women are secondary, thus competing with each other to be the most pleasing to men – to be the one who's noticed, the one who's pulled out and up, the one who finds favour and so gets access to the most power and the greatest sense of security.

This unequal yet unspoken dynamic presents as a phenomenon sometimes described as 'the Good Girl' – an unseen force that drives women to shape themselves to be the one who is most pleasing to men.

Modern sexism and the Good Girl

This Good Girl syndrome becomes part of the female condition (and condition is exactly the right word, for that is what it is – the product of conditioning) from the earliest age.

It's there from very early on in the soft and fluffy pink of the Babygro, and the hearts and flowers on the bedding for the cot. It's there in the dolls that little girls tuck up in their toy prams and in the plastic meals that they prepare in their toy kitchens. It's there in the pat on the head when they are told they have behaved well and 'what a good girl' they are.

It's there in the primary-school classroom where girls are encouraged to sit quietly and play nicely (while the boys are expected and allowed to rough and tumble and be naughty). As the psychologist Jill Weber describes it: 'Girls often sacrifice their independent discovery of who they actually are in order to live out the need to please others. In early childhood they are so good at the job of pleasing that they expect to hear they did a "good job", are "perfect", "nice", "beautiful", "well-behaved", "quiet".' The base setting is established: boys are there to please themselves but girls are there to be pleasing to others.

As girls become teenagers – and the underlying pull of the access to male power really kicks in – the Good Girl develops new dimensions concerned with pleasing men. How to be chosen? How to be the most appealing? How to look how boys like girls to look? How to behave in a way that charms and pleases and engages but never challenges or threatens? Here we see girls – who up until puberty have skipped (quite literally) through life in a largely unselfconscious way – begin to tread carefully, to hold themselves back and shape themselves (again, quite literally) according to what pleases: to start to wear make-up and 'become obsessed with the perfect look', to begin to feel anxious about not just who they are but how they are – how they look, how they should appear, how popular they are or aren't. Appearance becomes as, if not more, important than action. Unnoticed and unknowingly, girls become unwitting victims of the stealthy forces of sexism.

As teenage years progress, the next stage on the Good Girl life course is to please by becoming the ideal partner – a persona that ranges from the blow-up-doll sex object willing and ready to please her man to the high-pony nice girl who will always oblige. At the top of the tree (which is where sexism meets racism and classism) is the well-heeled white girl – pure, blonde, well-mannered, blemish-free. She is the one most likely to be chosen: always pretty, always passive and always (even outside Europe and the US) white.

Later, of course, the need to please, and to conform to what is useful and attractive to men, presents in the ideal of the Perfect Mom, and the characteristics that the Good Girl must now exhibit become pleasing in another way. To be perfect, she must now be organized, consistent, patient, kindly, comforting and constantly trying to keep people from being angry or from fighting. She must be the foundation parent, the one who takes responsibility for everyone and everything in the family in a way that ensures their load remains as light and carefree as possible. In addition, she must play a legion of other roles: she must be the perfect partner, volunteer at the kids' school, look after her parents, keep fit, bake cakes and keep the house sparklingly clean and 'to-do-list' orderly.

In addition – but never in conflict with all that unpaid labour – she is also allowed to 'have it all' and work: a series of shifts, a job in a caring profession, or a 'high-powered career girl' – it's all now in her grasp. Throughout it all her appearance must be maintained: she must carry on being hot, she must have a great toned body, she must stay well dressed and fashionable, she mustn't overeat. And above all else, she must stay smiley and soothing and sunnily indulge the inability in others to take responsibility for themselves.

She must never make time for herself (unless it involves the further pursuit of any of the above) or she is 'given' some special, one-off 'me-time' by those she cares for.

Then, of course, these Perfect Moms role model perfection for their daughters and the next generation of Good Girls is created: always putting their needs last, always ensuring their appearance and their personalities please others, always with an eye on how to win favour so that they too can one day fulfil the role of Perfect Mom. And so it goes around, on an infinite loop.[1] Always perfect, always pleasing (but please: never, ever mumsy).

In her job, the Good Girl is hard-working and eager to please: always prepared, always worried that what she's done is not enough. In all probability, if there's a low-paid (aka low-worth) job that involves looking after or serving others – child-minding, cleaning, caring, cashiering, clerical work, call-centre – she'll be the one doing it. She's the beautiful PA guarding the power of the creative director; she's the highly able executive who, on average,[2] gets paid 17 per cent less than a man; she's the dutiful deputy to the charismatic front-of-house CEO. She's the one in the meeting who notices the coffee isn't there for the guest and offers to see where it's got to; she's almost certainly the one who's in the kitchen actually making it. And, of course, she's Lynda from Human Capital Management tirelessly organizing the female network on top of her day job.

Then – and you'll be very relieved to hear this as it's exhausting just to recount the twisting-up, relentless, perfection-seeking narrative that being the Good Girl entails – once the children are grown and away, the Good Girl can begin to ease up. Her 'usefulness' in pleasing men, having children and raising a family reduces. As she enters her fifties, her value and worth are almost gone and she can fade quietly off the scene. Her exhausting, relentless, perfection-seeking, multi-tasking, never-ending work is done. She has 'had her day', is 'over the hill' and can now 'let herself go'. In middle age, the Good Girl disappears and retreats into dotage and greyness. Good-bye, Good Girl (don't feel too sad, the Good Girl won't mind; she's used to being recessive to the main act and doing what the narrative requires of her).

To make quite sure that the Good Girl stays in her box, doesn't stray from the path of righteousness, sticks to her bell-curve story line – and to add just that little smidgeon of fear and fist to the stealth of the velvet glove – a countercultural narrative is also in operation: the narrative of the 'bad girl', the rebel, the misfit who doesn't stick to the script. This girl – typically depicted as dark-haired, dark-skinned, messy, mean, ugly or aggressive – is punished for her non-conformity. As a young girl, she'll be the isolated lonely one who gets left out; as a teenager, she'll be the plump, spotty misfit one who doesn't make the cheerleading squad; as an adult, she'll first be the slut, and then the slovenly mother, and finally the unhinged spinster left only with her cats. When she challenges male authority, she becomes the humourless bitch, the ball breaker, or the who-does-she-think-she-is fool in the pant suit.

In the male discourse, rebellion is considered aspirational, noble and courageous – the rogue, the revolutionary, the fearless individual making his own way, living in a world where risk taking is to be encouraged and rules are made to be broken. In the Good Girl world, rules are to be abided by, risks avoided, and to rebel is to be difficult, bossy, to be 'getting above yourself' (note, the 'above'), or just a bit mad. The alter ego is always there in the background to keep the Good Girl on her mark, to warn her that it's easy to fall, and to insinuate that anything other than perfection is a disaster that will bring ridicule, humiliation, alienation and a barrage of dog-piling harassment across social media platforms.

Look around you and you can see the Good Girl narrative operating everywhere, usually accompanied by her badass 'let this be a warning to you' shadow. She's Cinderella (obedient, beautiful, dutiful, patiently waiting for her prince to come) and the Ugly Sisters (the clue is in the name). It's the Madonna (not that one) Whore dichotomy. It's Britney before and after. It was the Queen and Princess Margaret. It's now Kate Middleton (happy to be 'waity', always smiling, barely speaking, ever pretty, always thinner) and Meghan

Markle (the Other, devious, 'exotic', sharp-elbowed, above herself, cast out). In fact, it's more or less the basis of every single 'before and after' female transformation narrative.

Through every stage of her existence, the Good Girl personality must remain consistent: appealing but not too alluring, hard-working and achieving yet also passive and agreeable, capable yet also willing to be told, engaging and pleasing but never, ever too challenging. As a result of this competing tightrope of demands and expectations, the Good Girl is caught in a perpetual circle of self-doubt – on the one hand 'Am I (good) enough?' and, on the other, 'Am I too much?' And with all of that come the issues of self-esteem and self-confidence – particularly around body image – that we see throughout female lives. To be and become the Good Girl is a never-ending quest towards perfection and a male-authored ideal, with dreadful consequences threatened for those who fall off the rails.

This understanding of power relations between men and women explains not only the dominant definitions of female personality – soft, caring, kindly, soothing, agreeable, passive – but also the dominant mores of female presentation. To be chosen, and to be Good, women must know what 'pleasing to men' looks like; and to know what that looks like, they must be seen (and see themselves) through male eyes.

And so we get to 'the male gaze' – the phenomenon originally described by Laura Mulvey whereby 'the visual arts and literature depict the world and women from a masculine point of view, pre-senting women as objects for male pleasure'.[3] The Good Girl is taught to look at herself as men will see her, and, in pretty much every case and situation, to then adapt herself according to his ideal and perspective. The gaze is male and the lens, all too often, is critical.

Marketing made the Good Girl just perfect

From the word go, the methods of marketing to women were completely predicated on seeing the world according to the unbalanced power relations of man as higher authority and woman as Good Girl. And, when you look at the origins of modern consumer marketing, and the era in which it was forged, it's easy to see why: marketing is – quite literally – a man-made construct. Created in the white heat of the Good Girl years of 1950s America, where David Ogilvy built an entire advertising empire out of the startling insight that 'the consumer isn't a moron – she's your wife', marketing was created at a time when only men held the power. As a result, the base-setting models of marketing were, by default, developed from the male perspective and so subject to that bias described so brilliantly in 1949 by Simone de Beauvoir in *The Second Sex*: 'the representation of the world as the world itself is the work of men; they describe it from a point of view that is their own and that they confuse with the absolute truth.'

As the fifties and the sixties went by, and the early base-setting assumptions turned to accepted techniques and proven practice, marketing began to really stand up and promote the Good Girl ideals. And it was always an ideal – definitions, aspirations and presentations that sought perfection, and under which good enough was never good enough. Perfection (and the endless effort to achieve it) should be both the pursuit and the aspiration: complexions should be 'flawless', homes should be 'ideal', surfaces should be 'shining', dishes should be 'sparkling', the look and the figure should always be 'perfect' (and particularly perfect looking), the model girl was exactly that – a model to be followed and emulated.

Again, it's really easy to see why it was so convenient for marketing to project these Good Girl ideals: being and becoming a Good Girl is a construct that is absolutely replete with emotional needs and, as we all know, there's nothing that marketing likes more than a juicy set of needs. The never-quite-good-enough, always-room-for-improvement, don't-stop-trying-or-you-might-derail cultural narrative offers thousands of marketing opportunities: make your bathroom cleaner, make your baby safer, make your washing whiter, make your skin whiter (yes, that was – still is, in fact – a thing), make the toilet smell nicer, make your eyes look bigger, make your skin look brighter, make yourself look younger, make your hair look glossier, make your breakfast more nutritious, make your kids cleverer, make your heart healthier, make your body fitter, make your home happier.

The too-much-too-little-but-never-quite-right perfection-seeking narrative was also exceptionally helpful in fuelling market development. Because all those needs can never be met, and because the ideal is one that can never be realized, the pursuit is therefore constant and the search for perfection endless: New Season, New Look, New Improved Formula, New for Summer, New for Winter, New Year New You, New In, Blue Is the New Black.

And, most helpfully of all perhaps, the power relations that determine the Good Girl allow the brand to assume the authority: by operating on a higher plain, knowing best and better, flagging up the need and then providing a solution to it, the brand was able to position itself as the solution. Thus, brands were able to claim a role and advantage for themselves, to build on the 'we know more and best' principles to create competitive advantage, develop expertise and so drive loyalty.

Before long, the whole way that audiences were defined, sectors delineated, brands developed and communications produced was inextricably entwined in this gendered view of the world, where the brand claimed the (male) authority and the female audience was on receive, waiting to be told.

We have already seen how, from the moment baby girls came

into the world they were treated as separate: categories were divided into pink and blue, For Her and For Him. Barbies were for girls and Action Men were for boys. Girls had the Little Princess's Palace; Boys had the Knight's Castle.

As they grew into teenagers, the modern beauty category came into being providing ways and means towards the young Good Girl ideal. And the way that ideal was drawn was strikingly narrow: slim, pretty, youthful, bright, pure, without blemish, and always white. Make-up existed to hide imperfections and 'create a flawless face'; lipsticks were named Lolita; blushers (the clue was in the name) were there to make skin fuller and flusher; a whole world of hair care offered ways to transform your hair from lifeless to luscious.

Later, marketing played whole-heartedly to and on the Perfect Mom and the Perfect Housewife, selling images of smiling babies and domestic bliss, and promises of whiter washes and ways to keep 'hands that do dishes as soft as your face'. A media-buying audience was categorized 'Housewives with Kids'. Cleaning products – often given masculine names and superpower charac-ters like Mr Muscle and Flash – came to women's rescue as they sought (always happily, of course) to achieve a whiter, brighter, cleaner, better, kinder home. And, of course, in those days, it was whiter in every sense: other ethnicities were nowhere to be seen as beginghamed housewives with springy blonde hair represented the ideals of the era.

Meanwhile, anything that was female but that wasn't pleasing to the male agenda was hushed up and hidden: feminine hygiene was a category referenced in coded whispers and coy euphemisms like, well, 'feminine hygiene', in airtime bought to shield the subject from wider view.

The binary idea that men held the power and the authority while women took secondary place was further played out in entire cat-egories that operated on the basis that there were 'some thing(s) for the ladies' and other (more serious and important and more worldly) things for men. The automotive sector was an almost entirely male preserve, concerned with power, machinery and drive; women, if included, were either draped across the bonnet or there, quite literally, as passengers. Financial services was another field in which the primary audience was assumed to be male and so able to deal with the grave business of money, while women were barely considered, and, if shown, cast either as splurgers or overcome with delight at the purchase of some shoes.

In electronics, telecoms, alcohol, technology and tobacco, the dynamic was the same: male purchases were presented as big and powerful and primary; female purchases were, by contrast, entry-level, dumbed-down, happy to be given a lighter or smaller or sweeter (in both senses) version that wouldn't trouble their pretty little heads too much. We had the full-strength Marlboro Man and the more demure Virginia Slims, 'slimmer than the fat cigarettes that men smoke . . . tailored to fit your hands, your lips, and your purse'; we had pints for men and smaller bubbly sweet drinks like Babycham and Woodpecker for the ladies; Coke was 'The Real Thing' for men, Diet Coke was only for women; we had man-sized tissues; we had big chunky Yorkie fuelling the tough work of truck drivers and lighter, breakable Flake for available women in silk negligees sitting on windowsills.

This binary view of the powerful and worldly and important belonging to men, and the trivial and domestic belonging to women, was further advanced both by the media and by the way in which it was organized. TV channels on both sides of the Atlantic were male-owned and run. Burly anchormen reported the news agenda. In newspapers across the globe, the main body of the paper was dedicated to worldly subjects, the closing pages dedicated to sporting interests, with subjects that were assumed to be 'women's interests' cordoned off and given their own minority sections in a spare corner. In the US, the *New York Times* had a women's section entitled 'Food, Fashion, Furnishing and Family'; in Britain, the *Sun*'s famous Page 3 model (retired only in 2015) signalled to male tabloid readers that women were there for their pleasure. Women were given their own separate media – *Woman's Own, Yours,*

Woman's Realm, Woman and Home, Good Housekeeping, Ideal (there it is again) *Home, House and Garden* – magazines invariably owned by men but written by women for women about – well, the titles say it all.

Across the board, male voices dominated and determined and assumed a masterful authority – and when talking to women, brands adopted the same in-charge and in-control manner. They spelt out what 'good' looked like, told women what they needed or lacked and cast them as vacant beings ready and eager to be told (and then sold). In beauty, women were told 'that Mr Max Factor of Hollywood created this perfume for you'; in tobacco, the audience were given a pat on the head and told 'You've come a long way, baby' (note the 'baby'); in categories as diverse (not that sort of diverse, we're still in the twentieth century, remember) as shampoo, nappies, san-pro, even tea, the male voice took on a serious explanatory tone to deliver 'the science bit' cutaway; men in white coats with rich, strong, commanding (think about those words) voices delivered the end line and, with it, the final say.

In a true story so revealing that it is almost parabolic, L'Oréal's famous end line began life in 1973 when a young female feminist copywriter, Ilon Specht, grew tired of the male-pleasing tropes of the haircare category:

> [T]he men in the office would treat you like a little girl, because that's how they liked you to act, like you looked up to them and needed them . . . in a moment of anger, I thought it's not about men, it's about ourselves. It's not for *you* that we're going to do our hair. I'm not making my hair so you should like me.[4]

Fuelled by her anger, she wrote a campaign from the perspective of the female customer with the end line 'Because I'm worth it'. Quite quickly, however, the campaign was changed: the female perspective switched to become male, and the 'I' in the end line was modified so that it became 'Because *you're* worth it'. The moment when the female customer was in charge and acting with agency was short lived: the brand seized back control, taking back the high ground and determining what beauty looked like and what women needed to do to achieve it.

As the twentieth century rolled on, and marketing became increasingly technical, the addiction to Good Girl thinking became more and more hard-wired into the way things got done. In fact, it could be argued that marketing was, if not the author, then at the very least the illustrator of the Good Girl: the first to make her flesh, turning her from an abstract fuzzy cultural idea that existed in the ether into a real, living image looking out from every billboard and magazine cover. The Good Girl archetypes were the perfect shorthand to employ in the limited thirty-second broadcast TV medium; the endless Good Girl depictions and quests for perfection offered the ideal images and content for female magazines and retail formats. As the concept played out in full technicolour and the images proliferated, the Good Girl became ever more set and ever more ingrained into the way that marketing worked.

Marketing Man was in charge

And so it was that, when we joined the advertising industry in the final decade of the twentieth century, the Good Girl base settings – in all their various age and life-stage forms – were well and truly embedded into the way that marketing worked and communications were developed. In fact, in many ways, the end of the century represented what might be described as the Golden Age of the Good Girl: a time before the dual disruptions of fourth-wave feminism and digital media – when the existing models reigned supreme and reached their height.

Men controlled the conversation

At the time, broadcast media ruled the day – and was almost exclusively male-owned and run. Six big media conglomerates controlled almost every major media and news outlet in the US and they were (and in most instances still are) all run by men: Rupert Murdoch's News International; the Redstone family's National Amusements, Viacom and CBS; Disney, which was run at the time by Michael Eisner; Time Warner (Jeff Bewkes); Comcast (Brian Roberts); and Sony (Kazuo Hirai). Almost certainly as a direct result, men prescribed and dominated the cultural conversation and the world view: in 2000, the 'Who Owns the News?' study conducted by the Global Media Monitoring Project found that, across the world's news media, women represented just 18 per cent of news subjects, while men accounted for 82 per cent.

And it was the same in film. According to the Celluloid Ceiling study, of the top 250 grossing films in 2000, women comprised just

19 per cent of all directors, producers, writers, executive producers, editors and cinematographers: 89 per cent of directors, 86 per cent of writers, 98 per cent of cinematographers, 81 per cent of editors and 76 per cent of producers were men. In the UK, only 13 per cent of newspaper editors (in other words, probably no more than three or four) were women.

Macho biggest-is-best business

But it wasn't just in media and popular culture that male voices and approaches dominated: the whole world of business was, in those days, still overwhelmingly masculine in composition and macho in character. It was the end of the century and the dawning of a new-millennium era of buoyant hope in market possibility. After a period of dull and sluggish growth in the 1990s, a new world opened up as globalization and a belief in unfettered markets promised the dawn of an era of possibilities and opportunities for all. Market deregulation, global growth, competition and the rapid rise of new technologies would benefit us all: liberated markets would unleash competition and consumption, the fittest companies would survive and thrive, profits and possibilities would trickle down and the rising tide would lift all ships.

This new era of growth and possibility, with companies released to compete to dominate the world, was spearheaded (a nice bit of male vocabulary there just to create the mood) by businesses that were overwhelmingly male in their leadership. In Britain, at the time, there were just eleven female executive directors of FTSE 100 companies: that's eleven amongst almost four hundred men. No British woman had ever headed a big British company. In 2003 a large study of British quoted companies found that 65 per cent had no women on their board at all. In the US, in 1995, the Glass Ceiling Commission appointed by the federal government found that 95 per cent of senior managers were men. We worry a lot – and hear a lot – about the number of women leading major companies today, but in 2000 only 3 per cent of the Fortune

500 companies had a female CEO. (It's now just under 25 per cent, you'll be pleased to hear.)

The dominance of men in corporates – combined with an economic paradigm besotted by the possibilities of free markets, unfettered growth and global expansion – fuelled corporate cultures that favoured what were often described at the time as 'masculine' leadership attributes – confidence, decisiveness, assertiveness, independence, self-reliance and a highly competitive outlook. Less was never more, bigger was always better, biggest was best of all and good always aspired to become great. A new, turbocharged, out-with-the-old culture of expansion ruled the waves: banks became as big as nations, local strove to become global, national rapidly networked up to become international, and companies like Walmart and Tesco chased growth by becoming 'master brands' that sought to extend not just into new geographies but into new markets and sectors.

Women emerged in value as an audience

But while the expansionist economic paradigm, and the corporates that led the charge (doing it again) were overwhelmingly male, this didn't mean that women were out of the picture and played no part in these new equations. In fact, during the final years of the twentieth century there was a growing sense that women could be of increasing value to business – both as an external consumer audience and as an internal audience of employees.

The booming sense of onwards-and-upwards growth – and the expansion and extension into new markets – brought with it a growing recognition that women were becoming a target audience that any progressive, forward-looking organization should consider. It has always been received wisdom that women were the minority audience in most high-value categories (aka the male preserves of automotive, financial services, real estate, technology, utilities and consumer electronics) but accounted for 80 per cent of purchases in the minor 'small ticket' categories of household and health and beauty.[5] As the century came to an end, however, the received wisdom began to be challenged as a mechanic in the no-holds-barred growth agenda. A number of studies (with titles like *The Power of the Purse* and 'The She-conomy' that now seem astonishingly condescending) demonstrated that women were becoming an audience of growing affluence and growing agency in categories that had for so long been considered the preserve of men.[6] As markets boomed, and consumers matched and fuelled the more is more and bigger is better ethos of the age, the new possibilities of women as an audience began to be examined.

A valuable – but secondary – audience internally too

Within organizations, there was also a growing interest in women as an internal audience. The dynamic, modern, success-is-good-for-all business began to recognize that women were a source of competitive advantage – both in terms of 'the talent pool' and as a way of burnishing their modern and progressive credentials. A whole forest of studies at the time (and many of you will have read them) focused on the special subject of 'women in business' and revealed that the macho culture of many businesses – and the employment practices that went along with them – was not good for women. In fact, and worse still, women were having to twist themselves out of shape in order to fit within businesses, and were often 'dropping out' when this all became too much. As a result, it was widely recognized that businesses needed to 'do more' for women: in fact, it became something of a signature of modernity and enlightened thinking for businesses to have a special programme to 'look at women'. Ripple dissolve to a huge series of well-intentioned 'initiatives', research studies, internal interviews, HR reports, female networks, mentoring schemes, off-sites and away-days that set out to understand how businesses could and should 'do more' for their female employees.

The business of 'doing more' for women was not without its complexities and resistances when reaching out to them as customers either. As organizations began to think about women as a target audience and how they might reach out to them, they were concerned about wanting to do that in a way that did not upset the apple-cart of their existing male audiences. We were often called in as 'special guests' to all-male meetings with agency clients to discuss how a brand could develop a new product or service to appeal to the increasingly affluent audience of women (but without 'weakening' the brand). Almost invariably the discussion descended into concerns around threat rather than opportunity. Male brand managers worried that the effort would mean the brand would 'go all soft and fluffy' or would in some way dilute its powerful male values and attributes. Or the meeting bought up a new purchase dynamic that was now worrying marketers: the 'female handbrake'. This was a threatening phenomenon whereby women were now actually influencing men in what to buy – and what not to buy. Brands, particularly in high-ticket, technology and machine-based categories, were 'being held back' by women exerting their influence (aka being nagging killjoys) and marketers were keen to know what to do to 'release' (aka silence) their objections.

Gender thinking underscored 'equality' and difference

The difficulty of adapting primarily male structures and models to 'do more' for women led to an approach to gender that became fashionable around this time: to understand how to 'do more' for women meant understanding the ways in which they were seen as different from men. This approach – buoyed up by third-wave feminism and its efforts to expose gender as a social construct – led to an examination of difference. Ripple dissolve to another forest of research studies, companies, theories and business models that – with the very best intentions – attempted to unpack gender difference. Men are from Mars and women are from Venus. Men are good at X (or rather XY) and women are good at XX. Women. Men. Different. Equal. (as the Equal Opportunities Commission strap line said at the time).[7]

Of course the problem with this approach – and yes, it's obviously much easier to see with hindsight – is that this focus on difference almost inevitably increased the boxed and binary nature of the way that men saw women (and, in some ways, women saw men). It was all too easy – coming on the back of decades of male authority and Good Girl thinking – for what were described as 'masculine' characteristics to be (and so remain) dominant and for the characteristics described as 'feminine' to be cast (yet again) as secondary and lesser. Very quickly, and with the best of intentions, the thinking can consolidate, and actually give licence to, the sort of approach that Julia Serano later described as 'oppositional sexism': 'the assumption is that masculinity is strong while femininity is weak; that masculinity is tough, whilst femininity is fragile; that masculinity is rational while femininity is irrational; that masculine is serious while femininity is frivolous; that masculinity is functional while femininity is ornamental'.[8]

At the time it certainly consolidated – under, ironically, the banner of being open and enlightened – structures that said major markets were for men (but should now 'do more' for women) and models of leadership that said the major attributes were male (confident, decisive, resilient, assertive, independent, self-reliant), but there was now a place, at least, for the feminine (expressive, intuitive, collaborative, loyal, empathetic).

Marketing told girls how to be good

And nowhere was this major-minor, men-in-charge (and women in support) dynamic more obvious than in the culture of marketing and ad agencies. At the time, almost every single ad agency was owned, set up and run by a man – and, typically and tellingly, bore the name of the man or men who'd done so. Ogilvy and Mather. Doyle Dane Bernbach. J. Walter Thompson. Young & Rubicam. Bartle Bogle Hegarty. Saatchi and Saatchi. In agencies, these male leaders called the shots – famous male CEOs ran the businesses and even more famous (often infamous) male creative directors dictated the culture. The cult of the male creative director was evident in the way that every agency operated: he was the one, sitting at the top of the tree and often guarded by a team of beautiful PAs, who had absolute authority over the work that the agency produced (and often over the clients the agency would work with). His word was more or less law, his behaviour, however bad, was not only tolerated but also frequently lionized as the stuff of agency legend, and his ego and reputation were allowed (in fact, often encouraged) to reign supreme. In the creative departments that he ran, the culture (and so the work that was produced) was overwhelmingly masculine; in 2000 the IPA conducted a special 'Women in Advertising' study in the UK and found that only 17 per cent of agency copywriters were women and just 14 per cent of art directors. There was only one female creative director in the whole industry. At the agency where we worked, there was only one female creative team; they were called 'The Seamstresses', were given a tiny office off to the side of the main floor, were routinely handed the boring briefs that none of the men felt they wanted to touch, and no one (including them and us) really thought anything of it.

Meanwhile, women in agency culture performed the classic Good Girl support roles: they took care of the (usually male) clients, they organized all the admin and hassle of TV production and they operated in secondary positions – the same IPA study found that only 9 per cent of those operating at senior management levels were women.

Unsurprisingly, the all-male creative teams naturally made worlds in their own image and through their own lens. And they then employed other men to execute their 'vision' – the overwhelming majority of directors and photographers of commercials (particularly those advertising the big fashionable brands) were male. As a result, the male gaze determined almost everything, from how propositions were developed and how briefs were written to how creative ideas were conceived, cast and produced.

And the award goes to . . . men

Not only that, but male tastes and preferences determined and dictated the creative standards in the industry as a whole: the ad industry was (and still is) obsessed with awards and, in those days, the juries were almost all male and the awards for the most admired and respected work were, surprise surprise, almost all in male categories. An analysis of the Cannes Grand Prix winners from 2000 to 2006 showed only one winner in what could be described as a 'female' category (Ikea); the other 134 awards were all for male brands in male categories.[9]

In fact, in 2000, the ad-land topography could hardly have been more male. The campaign of the year was for Budweiser and was called 'Whassup!' You might remember it – it was actually revived recently when the world was in lockdown – it basically consisted of a bunch of American blokes screaming 'Whassup!' to one another down the phone. Not only did it win the top prize at Cannes, its catchphrase spread like wildfire across popular culture: footballers adopted it as a yell of triumph when they scored; men shouted it to each other when they met and made calls; Homer Simpson used it in an episode of *The Simpsons*.

Another big hit that year – both in industry awards and in pop culture – was the gorgeous 'ideal woman' forty-seconder for Lynx deodorant. This ad featured a parade of hot male-pleasing women uttering words that men can only dream of hearing. So a stunning brunette purred: 'Oh no, if I'd wanted foreplay I would have asked for it,' as another, similarly succumbing to 'the Lynx effect', cooed: 'Do you mind if my best friend joins us?' Even dreary old banks got in on the big manly act: Barclays Bank won a bunch of awards with a series of blockbusters featuring a big theme and big names and directed by one of the biggest directors, the late Tony Scott. The ads depicted various stars, including Sir Anthony Hopkins, musing on the theme of 'bigness' to fit with the new Barclays end line 'A big world needs a big bank'.

In those days, too, marketing directors were almost always men and the relationship between them and their agencies was forged around those bastions of male bonding: golf and booze. One of the highlights of the London agency scene in the 1990s was a boxing event, where an audience – made up mainly of men – sat in black tie cheering on their favoured pugilist. A few women would occasionally be invited but they were typically the Good Girls in the agencies – the ones who understood that their real role was to go along with the men.

So, as we went into the twenty-first century, the ultimately useful and entirely pleasing binary ideas of men and women were still deeply hard-wired into the way that things were seen and said and done. In fact, an open expression of the idea that men were one thing and women were another was considered fashionable: a liberated post-modern recognition of male and female difference that could allow the strengths of each to come to the fore.

The real thing was male

As a result, the idea of pink and blue was still a thing. Mobile phones were sold in pink versions; children's clothes and toys were rigidly gendered; Dell had a cutesy pink laptop called Della; in booze, there were drinks called Skinnygirl cocktails and Vixen Vodka; brands like Sheila's Wheels co-opted pinkness to sell motor insurance to women. It was all done with a knowing, post-modern, reclaiming-the-girl wink, often employing 1950s and 1960s housewife imagery but playing out and standing up the same old binary 'for him'/'for her' script nonetheless. There was even the objectionable practice that developed during this time that became known as 'shrinking and pinking': brands from technology to telecoms to razors to guns (it's true, and it's still out there – google 'pink gun') produced a smaller version of the 'real' thing decked in some sort of pink or flowery colour code, and then sold it at a premium as something 'special', 'just for her'. As the journalist Liz Plank says: 'men's razors being both cheaper and sharper than women's razors is patriarchy in a nutshell'.[10]

Once we were working on content for a credentials meeting in the hope of being asked to pitch for *The Economist*, and one of the hoops the agency was asked to go through was to develop recommendations on how *The Economist* could reach out to women. The male creative director we were working with at the time (names redacted to protect the guilty) was insistent that the answer to this challenge was to turn the colour of the very famous red and white ads to pink and white. Even at the time, the suggestion was considered debatable, but the discussion about whether or not it should be put forward went on for several days, and many hours, as we battled to get it taken off the table ('Bloody difficult women; no sense of humour . . . I'm beginning to wonder if they're really right for the agency . . .').

Male-pleasing ideals prevailed

In those days too, the dominant depiction and presentation of the Good Girl was still extraordinarily narrow. In project after project we encountered audience descriptions that were as restrictive as they were repetitive. Young women were depicted with depressing regularity as very slim, very pretty, very white and very heterosexual; airbrushing and photoshopping were the default setting as women were changed to become more slender, more desirable and sometimes even more white versions of themselves. A study conducted in 2004 found that many of the models shown in TV ads and in other forms of popular media were approximately 20 per cent below healthy body weight[11] – thus meeting the diagnostic criteria for anorexia. The camera almost always adopted the male gaze: looking at women through male eyes, and seeing them not as themselves but as men like to see them. In fact, one piece of analysis found that 'in 1983, women were depicted in a sexual way in 30 per cent of the ads, and in 2003 it was 78 per cent. It's obvious from the previous research that the sexual depiction of women in magazine ads has increased over time.'[12]

During those years, that powerhouse of male fantasy – Victoria's Secret – was still going strong and represented, with almost uncanny accuracy, the Good Girl story. Models vied for the honour of walking the Victoria's Secret catwalk wearing a soft porn lingerie set and angel wings (what else would a Good Girl wear?). Only the goodest girls – that is to say the ones operating in starvation mode, exercising furiously on an empty stomach – got to be an angel (could the nomenclature have been any more telling?). At the end of the show the girl who had been most Good – the thinnest, the sexiest, the one who looked like the least likely to answer back – got to wear the wedding underwear. This was the highest prize Victoria's Secret could promise: the security and safety of marriage and male favour.

In creative brief after creative brief we'd see women reduced to a box described as 'housewife with kids', with an accompanying narrative explaining how 'she' was a busy, multi-tasking mother, juggling to keep work, family and home running without mishap. Sometimes a more 'enlightened' brand would develop this description to bestow on her the grand title 'CEO of the household' – putting her in control, but only of the domestic space. Occasionally, a 'career woman' would be shown, laptop under one arm, toddler under the other, hair still swishing, skin still glowing, personality still pleasing. But showing a woman at work was rare: in a meta analysis conducted in the US that looked at commercials over a thirty-year period from 1980 to 2010, women were shown at work in only 4 per cent of commercials.[13] Women were twice as likely as men to be in commercials for domestic products, and men were twice as likely as women to appear in ads for non-domestic categories. Another study revealed that 73 per cent of advertisements that featured women showed them as decorative or in a role where they appeared only to enhance the product.[14]

The critical eye

Having set up the Good Girl ideal to their audience, the promises and propositions of most brands then focused on how to achieve that ideal – what women needed to be or do in order to get closer to achieving the end. Almost inevitably, this resulted in propositions centred on perfection and problem–solution constructs: pointing up the problem in order to deliver the answer. The raison d'être of many brands – and the advertising narratives they inspired – centred on fixing problems, and so, almost by extension, fixing women. The brand explained to women where they were (going) wrong: how they could rid themselves of dark circles, puffiness, fine lines, wrinkles, eye bags, crow's feet, tired eyes; how they needed to fix 'concerns' – small and large pores; dark spots and hyper pigmentation, acne and blemishes, dry and dull skin.

Denial narratives

These 'you really need to fix this' narratives sometimes took an even more pernicious turn in categories that were concerned with aspects of the female body that weren't pleasing to men – in particular, in feminine hygiene. Here the propositions and presentations focused on the need to disguise and cover up – with the implicit suggestion that these uniquely female things were a source of shame and embarrassment. Denial narratives drove communications – white tennis skirts, roller-skating, leggings-wearing models, headlines telling us to 'slip on stilettos and rock your skinniest jeans' – were used to describe these facts of female life: things so far from the Good Girl ideal that they could barely be mentioned, let alone discussed. Mention of the menopause was taboo.

Women treated as vacant and dumb

When the construct of the brand was to set up the Good Girl ideal, and then tell women what they needed to fix in order to get closer to that ideal, it almost inevitably followed that the brand must speak in a way that assumed authority and demonstrated how and why it knew best. And, very often, this requirement to demonstrate superiority and authority resulted in a relationship that was – in the true meaning of the word – belittling: in order for the brand to become big, the audience had to become little.

Male authority voices

At its most mild, this presented as a prevalence of male authority voiceovers summing up the meaning of communication for the audience, or explaining what was happening over some sort of science-lab mnemonic. A study of 300 prime-time ads broadcast in Spain in 2005 found that 68 per cent had male voiceovers; another in Malaysia and Taiwan found that 81 per cent of voiceovers were male. At its worst, it presented as treating women as simpletons or children: vacuous, passive, credulous recipients who – like the blonde, smiling, agreeable, hair-swishing Jennifer Aniston of the L'Oréal ads – would happily be impressed with anything.

Very often the creative concepts we were developing in those days featured women who were so empty that they were basically there as vectors for the brand: gasping with gratitude at the product's performance, telling each other in awed terms about the merits of some cod-science formula, or more or less reading out the

proposition and benefit from the brief as if it was their own observation (with the inference that they were so gullible that they'd
believe and say what they were told). At worst, there was even a
trope referred to (in whispers) as 2Cs in a K – where two women sat
in a kitchen 'naturalistically' waxing lyrical to each other about the
power of some product or other. (You know the sort of thing.
Woman One: 'My stomach is really giving me trouble today.'
Woman Two: 'Why not try new X yoghurt? Now with added active
bacterial cultures! It's done wonders for me.' Woman One: 'I think
it's time I got new X today.' They both smile. Cue pack-shot and
happy soundtrack.) The K was for Kitchen and you can guess what
the Cs stood for.

Women – an audience grateful to receive

Alongside this presentation of women as grateful, gullible simpletons, who were eager and willing to be told, came another Good
Girl trope: the belief that the female audience was ready and eager
to listen, and didn't really require efforts to genuinely engage. In
our years in advertising, we were constantly struck by the fact that
work aimed at women tended to adopt a different focus and a different tone from that aimed at men. When the audience was female,
we were much more likely to see propositions that centred on
safety, on comfort, on harmony and on appearance; when it was
male, we typically saw promises of power, assertiveness, individuality, action and adventure. Equally, the executional treatments
often demonstrated a gendered view of life; female communications tended to be homebound and friends-and-family orientated:
male communications tended to be more out there in every sense –
in the world, on the stage – dramatized by production values that
create energy and excitement.

And then there were whole categories constructed along lines
that put men 'in charge' and where the Good Girl appeared only to
affirm or admire. Automotive was the classic. Here, the base-setting
assumptions continued to present women as secondary. The sector

was dominated by propositions that depicted male power – and cars as reflections of male drive. The end lines used to sum up male propositions in the category revealed how cars positioned for men were built around muscular promises of power, heroism, adventure and winning the race ('The Car in Front' (Toyota); 'Go Beyond' (Land Rover); the 'Ultimate Driving Machine' (BMW)). Cars that were positioned 'for women' were invariably treated as accessories, with the emphasis on 'cute' design, childish colours and 'girl-about-town' journeys.

Brands in the luxury goods space frequently played the same tricks, presenting women as beneficiaries of male largesse. Across high-end sectors – jewellery, watches, leather goods – women were shown not as purchasers but as recipients. Narratives frequently revolved around luxury products as trophies for a trophy or accessories for an accessory: product features emphasized beauty and good looks (and often small sizing) that were designed to enhance the beauty and good looks of the (mute and passive) recipient. By conspicuous contrast, brands for men in these categories typically revolved around propositions that underscored power and precision, supported by strengths in engineering and manufacture.

And then, and aptly as it will turn out – finally – there were all the categories and brands where the Good Girl didn't show up at all, simply because she was deemed to be too old to be of interest. As she passed fifty, the Good Girl, now no longer needed as a Perfect Mom, receded from the marketing picture: no longer really of interest, no longer really seen, no longer sexy. She might have made an occasional appearance, or you could put her in some ads that aired only in daytime when no one was looking, and, 'fine for her to appear in a cruise ad' – looking wistful and out-to-sea with a faint breeze of regret blowing in the wind – but basically get her out of here. She is now beside the point.

So, across the board, and right into the first decade of this century, the vast majority of businesses, the central practices of marketing and the major approaches in communications, followed brandsplaining principles that perpetuated the Good Girl. Almost all of it was unconscious, none of it was done in order to deliberately put and keep women down, all the rules were unspoken. However, had we had the cheek to actually speak (outspoken? very un-Good Girl) and to pull out the assumptions and practices that were really at play, had we – in fact – dared to write down the unwritten rules, then what might they have looked like?

Brandsplaining for beginners: a turn-of-the-century guide to marketing to women

Rule 1: Something for the ladies

As we approach the end of the twentieth century and look forward to the new millennium, the progressive leader may demonstrate his enlightened credentials by making conspicuous efforts to do more for women – both as customers and as employees.

In order to achieve this accommodation in a way that demonstrates understanding of both genders, it is helpful – and in line with current thinking on the subject – to consider men and women as different: men represent and retain power, authority, action and agency; women have separate and softer interests that tend to be concerned with people, emotion, nurture and support. These attributes may be usefully employed in support of the main 'feminine' act.

Rule 2: Set out ideals for women that are pleasing to men

To develop his products and propositions, there are a number of standard models that the marketer may select from: Dear Little Girl; Obedient Adoring Daughter; Hot, Sexy Body-Revealing Teen; Come-to-Bed Temptress; Perfect Mom; CEO of the Household; Washer and Cleaner and Cooker with a Heightened Sense of Duty; Multi-tasking Female Co-Worker Who Has It All But Still Gets It All Done; The Older Woman (if you must, but keep her hidden or have her doing the baby-sitting please).

The proposition should focus on the pursuit of perfectionism and achieving these ideal standards: the home that's always happy and harmonious; the skin that's always flawless; the wash that's always whiter; the towels that are always bouncier; the hair that's always glossier; the figure that's always shapely.*

NB: When casting, please ensure that all women have an agreeable personality and are of very limited character. Shows of agency or action will not be necessary. A token woman of colour may be included, but only on an exceptional basis.

Rule 3: Proceed to tell women where and how they fall short of said ideals

While it is up to women to fix their flaws, the brand is there to tell her what she needs to do in order to work towards the ideal. This may be achieved either by adopting a critical eye – consider highlighting flaws in her appearance, or implying her home or wash may be more dirty than it appears – or by gently inquiring, for example, if she can 'pinch an inch'.

Alternatively an encouraging pat on the head to support her in her quest for perfection may also be employed to useful effect (Ref: L'Oréal: 'Because you're worth it'; SMA: 'You're doing great').

NB: It is felt that certain particularly female-centric subject matter – for example menstruation – would compromise the ideals depicted and should therefore NOT be spoken about openly. Please use coded language and a carefree 'nothing-to-see-here' tonality in these categories. As with all female product sectors, the colour white (to suggest purity and cleanliness) should be heavily employed.

* We recognize that the bodies of real women do, unfortunately, invariably fail to conform to the required ideal. Please feel free, therefore, to manipulate body shape and image where necessary using Photoshop or other airbrushing technology to eliminate flaws and to reduce women's bodies down to the required form.

Rule 4: Make it clear that the brand knows more than the audience

In order to achieve credibility and advantage, the brand must assume a masterful position of authority: this requires the audience to be presented as secondary and knowing less.

A number of methods may usefully be employed in order to achieve this. Perhaps the most reliable is the exploitation of the 'male' world of 'science' in support of claims: typically this will involve a product formulation expressed in terms that echo scientific laboratory language. In executional terms, this may take the form of side-by-side product demonstrations; a 'science bit' cutaway in communications; a white-coated authority figure.

Alternatively, claims of the brand's 'power' can be very effective at asserting authority: this may be achieved via a forceful brand name, dynamic packaging design, or product demonstration.

As a minimum, masterful male voiceovers should be employed whenever the brand is 'speaking'.

The audience may be shown to be vacant, passive and receptive and to gratefully absorb the observations and proposition of the brand.

When dealing with complicated subjects that are outside the mainstream of female life (money, machines, business, et al.), it should be assumed that women know little and will need to be told. These subjects should therefore always be explained in simplistic terms or otherwise sugar-coated: consider how a trusted teacher helps an entry-level class to learn, or a kindly doctor speaks to a patient. Bright playroom colours and tones may also help the brand's authority to feel accessible.

Please note that this guidance differs from brands and communications designed to target men. Here, of course, the audience is more informed and worldly, and so willing listening cannot be assumed; attention-driving devices (such as humour, sophisticated production values, dramatic scenery, music, narratives that hold attention by featuring adventure and a hero's triumph) are therefore both permitted and encouraged. These techniques are not required to the same extent in female categories: domestic scenes, slice of life and images of people (particularly other women) should suffice.

Rule 5: Strongly signal to women what categories are for them (pink) and which are not (blue)

In line with societal norms, men should inhabit separate spaces from women and demonstrate different qualities. Male categories should focus on strength, power, authority, action and user status/ advantage; female categories should focus mainly on appearance, family nurture, household management/the domestic space and juggling the complexities of looking after others.

By contrast, female categories are not a relevant preserve of male audiences. Men need not feature in categories involving the domestic space, for example, and appearance should be considered a female concern. If any confusion arises, a simple rule of thumb may be followed: major categories = men = action, machines, business, money; minor categories = women = appearance, people, the domestic space.

Within brands, please keep products for men and women separate in order to ensure that 'the feminine' does not weaken the strength of our masculine propositions. Where a typically masculine product is targeted at women, it is advisable to offer a smaller, diluted and/or softer version of the original, and to use feminine aesthetics to signal 'for her'. It is often possible to charge a premium for these simple modifications.

Rule 6: Except under very exceptional circumstances, men should be the authors of all brands and communications intended for women

Men should be in ultimate charge at every stage of the communications development process, from 'owning' the brand and its proposition through to the creation and execution of advertising. While women may usefully be employed in service and support roles along the way (managers within marketing departments;

account handling teams in agencies; market researchers et al.), all judgements, decisions and sign-offs are – and must remain – in the gift of men, regardless of whether the category is female.

Creative directors, creative teams, directors of TV commercials and photographers should also be male and will therefore, either knowingly or unknowingly, employ 'the male gaze'.

On occasion, creative teams may require an understanding of the female audience to aid in their development of communications materials. Should this be the case, a female planner may traipse up to their office to deliver this understanding. Creative teams are free, at all times, to override her understanding with their own prejudice or singular point of view. During the visit, the female planner may comfortably be accommodated by seating her on an upturned bin.

Rule 7: Brand mastery

Finally, and as a helpful summary of the role of the brand and the desired relationship with the female audience: think 'mastery'. The aim is to assert the brand as the authority – in control, knowing better and speaking from a place of greater knowledge and understanding.

Unfortunately, this may occasionally demand that the audience be treated as ingénues – doubtful and concerned, ignorant and vacant, grateful or gullible. However, a shot showing her satisfaction with the product, the affirmation of another person (preferably male) or a pat-on-the-head end line should be sufficient to make her feel she 'is worth it'.

Where We Are Now

Brandsplaining – the New (But Not so Improved) Version

So here we are now, in the second part of the book. Everyone good? Twenty centuries of male dominance clearly explained and tucked away? The Good Girl model (not that sort – have you learned nothing!) read and recognized? The message about the role (and responsibility) of marketing in perpetuating the Good Girl received and understood? The base settings upon which modern marketing (and modern sexism), all clearly laid out? Slightly sarcastic rules read? Everyone still listening there at the back? Steve – are you and the rest of the guys still on board? Great, then let's move on. This part of the book is where we're going to look at where marketing went next: what changed as the twenty-first century settled in, what shifted in the years from 2005 to 2020, what genuinely moved forward, and what – when you examine it in the cold light of the current day – really remained the same.

We're starting this part here because it was at this point – around 2005 – that the challenges to the Good Girl constructs and the base-setting models that we've just described began in earnest. And it was at this point too that – whether by luck or by judgement (and we like to claim extraordinarily prescient judgement and searing foresight) – we left the agency world to set up our research company. As a result, we've been lucky enough to have seen and heard during this period, at first hand and up close, the change in how women see the world and their position in it. And, as we've researched numerous different markets and different needs, and conducted numerous different positioning, proposition and communications development projects, we've also been witness to the changing nature of the marketing designed to reflect those changes. We've seen the dawn of the marketing era often described as

49

'fempowerment' or 'femvertising' and we've seen what it has achieved and what it hasn't.

When we first set out, the changes and the challenges were there as signals that were still low level and far out, but over the intervening years we've seen them take root, build and come slowly in from the margins. Feminism – in its fourth-wave iteration – has gone mainstream, and it has been fascinating to witness many of the old limiting and diminishing ideas drop away in the process. It has been even more fascinating to see and hear women talk about the new and liberating alternatives that have arisen to take their place. Over the years that we've been researching, we have spent just over 4,000 hours talking to women about how they are experiencing this period of flux. In our efforts to find ways to market more successfully to women through it all, we've gone into their homes and listened as they've talked about their work, their relationships, their life stage and their ambitions. We've heard how they feel about themselves and their children, about men, about money, about how they appear and how they want to appear. We've asked them about what they hope for and what they fear. And we've listened while they tell us about being a child and having a child, about eating, about working, about ageing and about more or less everything in between.

So this part of the book is going to cover what we've seen and heard over those years and look at the place that we have now reached. If you read the top-line signals, at first sight that place looks like a sort of middle ground: there is progress, but there is also an apparently equal and opposite regression too. #Tradwives is a thing and there are Women for Trump – but there is also #MeToo and TimesUp and the well-attended women's marches across the world. The hyper-masculine leader stereotype still holds the keys to the kingdom in the world's superpowers but female heads of government in Germany and New Zealand show there is another way to do leadership. There are more women in boardrooms, and yet little movement at the lower pay scales for women in the supply chains of those same businesses. Jezebel continues but

Feministing has closed. There is Kim Kardashian but also Jameela Jamil. There's a huge growth in plastic surgery brands and there's also the body positivity movement. There is Brandy Melville and there is also Dove.

In this mixed, back-and-forth context we can point, as Steve did when we first met him, to the progressive signals and say – 'Hey it's all all right now.' Or we can point to the regressive ones and fall into despair. But neither of these positions is true to the whole reality of what's happening. It looks like a tangle. But on proper interrogation, the truth that emerges from beneath the flux, and outside the exceptional, is that most women – in the mainstream – do want the world to move away from the sexist ideas and Good Girl ideals described in Part One, and increasingly understand the serious limitations and, in fact, harm that they do to them. But . . . because in most of the component parts of their lives – culture, economics, business and, yes, marketing – men still maintain control, women's will and wishes are neither taken as seriously as they need to be, nor responded to in as meaningful a way as they deserve.

In marketing, what that response looks like is the continued prevalence of brandsplaining. Where the brand, despite all evidence to the contrary, still believes that it is in charge of the relationship it has with women and still deems it appropriate to explain things to them, even – and most notably in this 'fempowerment' era – to explain feminism to them. What we will show is that much of what gets produced by marketing either still conforms pretty rigidly to the Good Girl base settings (and is even sometimes a more extreme version of them), or puts on a veneer of change, but with the basic sexist settings continuing to lurk beneath.

And what we want to show you is that women see this. They've got your number, they have you bang to rights. They see past the exceptional cases and beneath the thin veneers, because they're the ones consuming the whole lot of it. Finally, we also want to show you that even the really brilliant cases like Dove, Libresse and Ariel that explicitly set out to challenge ideas that are harmful to women, can't provide a long-term answer to sexism in marketing.

This part of the book may, therefore, feel a bit gruelling to read, but go with it: it's here to provide a much better understanding of what's going wrong with marketing to women, in order to then point up the much more promising and exciting future that's going to be explored in Part Three. Because new female perspectives are now punching through from the margins and into the mainstream and will eventually shape a different-looking future for women and the businesses that serve them. In Part Three we are going to show how those green shoots can deliver on their promise for women – and, not just that, how they could make men's lives better too. But here let's assess where we are now, and why where we are in 2020 isn't going to be enough to connect with an ever more resourceful and even more self-sufficient female audience.

Women call out toxic femininity

When we begin our research discussions, we will frequently start our conversations by asking women to describe their hoped-for, their actual and their feared selves. The hoped-for self is them on their best day, or the person they like to think they are; the actual self is the person they are day to day; the feared self is them on their worst day, or the person they worry about becoming. The aim is to set the tone for the discussion – that we want the juicy insights, not just the smiling, all-is-well façade that we know the Good Girl demands women present to the world. Invariably, a number of respondents will well up as emotions bubble to the surface while they reflect on their hopes and fears, and the normal cheery exteriors will often come apart. Stories tumble out about financial pressures they've been under, disappointments in their love lives, managing troubled children or watching elderly parents fade away. But what's both remarkable and remarkably consistent is the underlying sense in the accounts that what they are is never good enough: when discussing and explaining their three selves, women almost invariably feel that their actual self is either too much or not enough, that their hoped-for self is 'silly' or largely unachievable, and that their feared self is like a black shadow, stalking them daily.

Women are palpably under a huge amount of pressure. The primary sentiment that gets expressed when we talk about how they experience their lives right now is a feeling of being 'overwhelmed'. And even more remarkable, this is as true for the rich as it is for the most cash strapped.

And we see it at every life stage. Up until puberty – and before the Good Girl conditioning has fully taken root – girls tend to power carefree through the world, but as early as the age of twelve, all that confidence suddenly drops away: 45 per cent of girls of this age say they feel they are not allowed to fail.[1] In the teenage years, the pressures build: from age sixteen, 52 per cent of girls say they are unhappy with their appearance.[2]

As the Perfect Mom stage of the Good Girl life kicks in, the pressure to conform to another ideal takes hold: according to a study conducted for an edition of *Time* magazine in 2017 entitled 'The Goddess Myth', 70 per cent of new mothers said they felt pressure to parent a certain way,[3] with the majority reporting disappointment or shame with how the reality actually played out. But it doesn't stop there: between the ages of thirty-five and forty-four women's stress levels apparently reach their height as they take on the Good Girl tasks of caring for parents, children, home and their work: 81 per cent of women surveyed at this life stage said they had felt unable to cope in the last year (compared with 67 per cent of men).[4]

When we listened to research in our old agency days, the concerns mothers voiced for their children largely revolved around threats to their physical safety – the usual accidents and scrapes a not quite fully developed person can get themselves into. Now when we talk to mothers their concerns are more to do with the mental health of their children and, in particular, the issues caused by the perfectionist narratives they see all around them. They discuss the pressures and impacts of social media on their daughters' self-esteem. At its most 'mild' this presents as a preoccupation with self-editing – often employing the old air-brushing tricks of twentieth-century ad agencies with Insta filters – to show their best lives and their best pose; at worst, it results in girls feeling so bad about themselves that they become not just unhappy but unwell.

We hear tales of mothers pleading with their daughters to eat just a little bit of food, and that refusing food is now a regularly presenting symptom of the stressed-out child. They discuss the steep rise in hospitalization for eating disorders (37 per cent between 2016 and 2019).[5] There is a palpable sense that their children are at the mercy of undermining forces, which are at best unthinkingly and at worst intentionally making them feel bad about themselves.

The too-much-but-not-good-enough narrative continues in work. The pressures to achieve perfection while dogged by the narrative of never-enough doubts explain many of the ongoing inequities that hold women back and down. The concentration of women in low-paid roles, women doing the majority of (unpaid) care work, the gender pay gap, the double bind, everything from the sticky floor to the glass ceiling to the fool in the pant suit – can all be explained, at some level, by this cultural narrative that casts women as secondary and in idealized roles originally developed to suit the needs of men.

And just in case the talk of cultural narratives and glass ceilings is giving the impression that these pressures are somehow theoretical or textbooky, let us just say – snap, even – that they really, really are not. Women express in almost all of our research discussions, regardless of the context or category, a series of continuous and lifelong anxieties that all, at some level, involve them tying themselves in knots in order to conform to Good Girl ideals and expectations: I'm a bad mum, I'm a bad daughter, I've been bad and fallen off the diet, I'm worried about him, I'm worried about her, how am I going to get 'it all' done, did I say too much, maybe I didn't do enough.

We recently completed a project on beds and bedding – an area where you might think the dominant themes would be peace and calm and resting easy. But no; what we heard was account after account of women lying awake at night, sleepless with the worry and the weight of having to be and do so much (and yet always, somehow, not doing enough). Even at night, the Good Girl cannot rest: sleep, it seems, is a feminist issue.

When we ask women to reflect on what has led to this sorry state, the impacts of the perfectionist narratives played out by brands and marketing are invariably mentioned. Marketing is held up as a major source of the pressure that they feel: most women – 63 per cent – say that they believe advertising is partly to blame for eating disorders, a third say they feel the body they aspire to is impossible for them to achieve, 94 per cent say that using women as sex symbols is harmful and 91 per cent feel that how women are seen in campaigns has a direct impact on girls' self-esteem.[6] Women see that marketing is actually creating problems for them and, increasingly, they are saying 'enough'.

What we are also seeing and hearing in our research is that women are recognizing too, in a much more active and angry manner, that the way ideas around gender play out for them is diminishing and/or limiting. Across all age cohorts, women recognize that traditional definitions of male and female strengths hold women back (i.e. the binary and often oppositional two-worlds ideas we described in Part One: men go to work, women stay home; men are bosses, women are support; men are primary, women are secondary). And while many women (75 per cent)[7] are still happy to agree that men and women have different strengths, they are increasingly questioning the role of nurture – the ways in which those strengths get twisted to suit the male agenda.

We often hear our female respondents complain that the strengths they are ascribed – and the tasks that go with those strengths – are the ones that are useful to the other people in their lives. By contrast, the strengths men get to own – and the tasks they therefore get to be in charge of – tend to benefit men themselves. Women feel they get cast as good at the boring, mundane and repetitive stuff (as much at work as in the home), where men have licence, through either learned or real incompetence at the boring things, to do what women feel is the more interesting or fun stuff. As one woman told us in research we were doing around holidays, 'I often feel used. The things I'm good at – organizing, juggling, noticing details – it's something everyone gets something out of. It keeps us all on track. But I don't get anything out of it, least of all thanks. I just get the jobs and the worry of getting it all done.'

Women tell us that they feel the 'talents' they are permitted don't have the same kind of impact as those of men. Their 'specialisms' don't lift the mood like a good joke does, or instil a buzz of excitement in the same way that manning the barbecue (in a comedy apron, obvs) is seen to do. The sort of tasks that they do – like carrying something exceptionally heavy from upstairs down to the kitchen – don't create drama and rarely even, in fact, get noticed. Women feel what they do is tiny and plodding by comparison to the out-there stuff of 'man's work': rather than create ripples, their talents keep the surface flat and still. Adding insult to this perceived injury, women report being criticized even as they are undertaking 'their' tasks. They are 'fussy', 'nagging', 'micro-managing' or 'pointlessly stressing themselves out'. 'Just chill,' they are told – which, as one woman described it, 'is basically code for saying what you care about is not worth caring about'.

More profoundly still, younger women are increasingly rejecting the idea of naturally occurring gendered strengths completely. When we talk to young women in our research they tell us – usually with an eye roll and an admonishing sigh – that the binary gender concept is blunt, inaccurate, limiting and jaded. In its place, they deploy a pick 'n' mix attitude to 'being a girl': a great love of skateboarding, a forensic understanding of the smoky eye, the commitment to writing in a unicorn-themed journal every evening and an ambition to study cardiac surgery does not, to them, seem in any way contradictory. Nothing belongs to boys and nothing belongs to girls. It's all up for grabs.

While older (over twenty-five) women find this idea a bit radical, almost half of them would agree that gender will become irrelevant in the future. And across all ages, 89 per cent of women would not choose gender as one of the characteristics that define them – in fact, they put it seventeenth in a list of twenty characteristics.[8]

And as, over the last fifteen years, we have seen and heard resistance to the idea that biology equals destiny grow, and grow bold, we've also seen and heard increasing recognition of the impacts and importance of intersectionality. While the concept of intersectionality has – in the wider political and cultural discourse – become increasingly caught up and contorted in left and right thinking, in our research we hear it expressed in much more practical and less academic terms. There's now a widespread and mainstream recognition that the monolithic idea of 'all men' and 'all women' is often unhelpful and shallow: respondents are quick to discern and describe the idea of different identities and to recognize that many marginalized and minority voices often get lost and diminished in a world – and particularly a marketing world – that still tends to focus on the white and the privileged.

So, over the last fifteen years of our research, and in the discussions we've heard and had, there's been building a recognition that the traditional views of gender are limiting, damaging and, for many women – particularly in those intersections – profoundly punishing. These feelings of frustration about the ways in which the world boxes and belittles women have been rumbling for many years but the reason that they have suddenly found new affirmation and voice is something that, when it first appeared, looked very innocuous – social media.

Social media has strengthened women's voices

It now seems longer than an age ago, but it is really only around the point that this part of the book begins – 2006 – that social media really became a thing, when Facebook and Twitter both became available to users throughout the world for the first time. And while it seems surprising that something so apparently slight as an emerging media channel could transform life for women, social media genuinely represents the most serious challenge at present – probably the most serious challenge ever – to the male stranglehold on the cultural and political conversation. Unlike the female-dominated channels of the past – let's go right back to the well, then the telephone, then coffee mornings and Tupperware parties – social media provides women with not just a way to discuss what matters to them between and amongst themselves, but to project what matters to them out to the rest of the world. As a result, the female lens on life has emerged out of the shadows and into the central fabric of life, infiltrating mainstream public consciousness and giving validity to the female perspective in a way that is utterly new and very, very exciting.

Women are the most avid early adopters of social media. Female users jumped on emerging social media platforms, which even in their earliest incarnations gave equal access to all voices and all interests. Between 2012 and 2014, 4G bedded down in everyone's increasingly overengineered smartphones, which further enhanced social media's ability to match and mirror the way women like to communicate and connect. The enhanced visual capacities of social media created a leap forward in female interest and use: image-led sites burgeoned, Pinterest overtook Tumblr and Instagram grew dramatically. Thirty-nine per cent of women use Instagram compared with 30 per cent of men, 41 per cent of women use Pinterest compared with 26 per cent of men. Weibo in China has broken through with female users as it shifted from a more text-based Twitter model to a multi-media platform.[9] And the new kid on the block TikTok is already skewing female.[10]

By 2010 women outnumbered men on all social media platforms except Twitter. This new level method of communication, expression and self-promotion nudges men out of the limelight and asks them to share it with a host of new female voices who are demanding to be heard. Social media reveals an angrier, more volatile, more challenging and all-round louder female population who aren't mediated and moderated by male curators to make sure they play by the Good Girl rules.

The Me Too movement is obviously the most high-profile example of the power of social media to pull the previously unrecorded or silenced into the spotlight. Almost every woman, girl and – as importantly – man and boy, is now familiar with the astonishing movement against sexual violence across the world in the days and months that followed the Weinstein revelations. High-volume and high-visibility images define the movement – *Time* magazine's 2017 Person of the Year cover featuring 'The Silence Breakers' (actor Ashley Judd, software engineer Susan Fowler, singer Taylor Swift, fruit picker Isabel Pascual, lobbyist Adama Iwu and an anonymous hospital worker); the line-up of actors and activists dressed in black at the Golden Globes. The MeToo hashtag has since been viewed more than 42 billion times by women across the world, resulting in an extraordinary set of consequences – an outpouring of pain, a number of high-profile men across different industries losing their jobs and facing justice, a surfacing of the previously unseen (or overlooked) extent of the problem, and, for ever more, a notice to men throughout the world: stop and think about your blithe treatment of women and the impact of your language and behaviour.

Social media offers women a place where they can experience sisterly affirmation and agreement. On traditional channels female views were, as we have discussed, cordoned off and relegated into a secondary place that came after the 'real' (male-owned) news and events of the day, but on social media they are pushing against open doors and receiving instant recognition. Social media has engendered a whole new vocabulary that beautifully expresses the micro-inequities women experience: gaslighting (characterizing a woman as mad if she's being disagreeable); mansplaining (you've got this one); manspreading (you can probably guess that one); even fridging (the use of murdered women as a cornerstone narrative in popular films and TV series, and their frequent subsequent disposal in fridges). The 'Mental Load' has emerged as an especially handy piece of vocabulary for women. You must look it up (only when you get to the end of this section). It's a cartoon strip by a French comic artist called Emma. In it she brilliantly summarizes the feelings of being overwhelmed that we described earlier, and the work that women do that goes unnoticed, unappreciated and, of course, unpaid. In these Covid-19 times, where women are shouldering so much of the coping burden, it's a concept that has never felt more relevant.

And, of course, with its endlessly elastic capacity for content, social media gives as much airtime to female interests as it does to male ones. In 2015 women's sport accounted for only 7 per cent of the total mainstream sports coverage.[11] A number of 'hot mic' incidents revealed the unhelpful way in which some in the industry think about women. Sports commentators on Sky seem to have particular trouble with their equipment. In 2011 a Sky commentator was caught off guard when he was heard to suggest that the female linesperson didn't know the offside rule: 'Why did they get a woman linesman? Someone's fucked up big time!' A similar 'live mic' error broadcast lewd conversations about women between sports commentators on the same channel. In that same year of strife for Sky Sports' PR department, Twitter was taking root and women were engaging fully with it. When the US women's football squad reached the World Cup final, a Twitter record was set with an unprecedented 7,196 tweets per second in the final moments of the game: a bigger engagement than the death of Osama Bin Laden.[12] The reaction to the match on social media blew the cover of mainstream sports broadcasters who asserted that no one was really interested in the women's game.

The growing use of social media by women over the first fifteen years of the twenty-first century means that the subject matter women care about has risen dramatically to the surface. YouTuber Zoella, a sweet-faced nineteen-year-old, went from an extremely modest 1,000 subscribers in 2009 to 11 million in 2020.[13] It gives airtime to disagreeable female voices, previously silenced on traditional channels, who are now arguing passionately against the need or the aspiration to be a Good Girl all the time.

And women's voices are being heard through more traditional channels too, precisely because they run directly counter to the expectations of how Good Girls behave. Beyoncé mused over leaving Jay-Z and makes her anger at his infidelity unequivocally felt in her album *Lemonade*, and performed a Black Panther inspired rendition of 'Formation' that felt radical in that bastion of (77 per cent white[14]) maleness – the Super Bowl. The US TV series *Orange Is the New Black* lined up an ensemble of women who overturned almost every principle of what a Good Girl looks and acts like. Even Disney tables Elsa, an anti-Disney princess, in *Frozen*. Female influencers began their journey in the 2010s to what is now power-brand status.

And now, and across the board, suddenly, 'outspoken' female voices are everywhere: in every bookshop when stories of fairy-tale princesses are eclipsed by stories of rebel girls; on every high street when pink T-shirts suddenly start to appear with the words 'Feminist AF' on the front; in the fearless girl standing up to the bull on Wall Street. Here in these very words in this very book.

The growing sense of rebellion and an increased propensity to call and speak out has been explored by Rebecca Traister in a brilliant book, *Good and Mad*, that looks at the revolutionary power of female anger, and how, over decades, the Good Girl ideals have effectively repressed and silenced anger and dissent with their requirement to be the soothing one and to 'Hold your temper and hold your tongue'. She describes how 'hard the powerful – very often the white and the male – have worked to shut up angry women . . . via silencing, erasure, and repression', but also shows how, when released, women's anger has, throughout history, had astonishing revolutionary power and driven immense social change. She welcomes in a new era of women's rage – afforded by social media – 'that could now become transformative political fuel . . . and a galvanizing force which, when harnessed, can change history'.[15] (Steve – are you OK there? You seem to be looking rather pale. Lynda – would you be so good as to get him a glass of water?)

But before we get too Pollyanna about the state of play here, let's register first that men do still control conversations held in the public domain. With surprising consistency, in fact, men continue to secure the most senior roles in almost all media organizations. In America's newsrooms, men outnumber women by three to one. In the UK press, three-quarters of all management jobs are occupied by men. In an analysis of news titles in the UK, male journalists' names fill 75 per cent of the front page by-lines.[16] Only 21 per cent of national newspaper editors are women,[17] and two-thirds of the journalists they employ are men. Across the world, men write 69 per cent of stories about politics and 67 per cent of the stories about crimes and violence.[18] Even when a subject is uniquely female in subject matter editors don't defer to the female perspective – 81 per cent of quotes in thirty-five US national publications about abortion, and 75 per cent of quotes about birth control, are made by men. On the subject of women's rights, 70 per cent of the quotes were given by men.[19] Men are also the authors of most of what gets aired in film and TV. In 2019 out of the top one hundred grossing films, only 12 per cent of the directors were women, one in five of the writers, 2 per cent of the cinematographers and 19 per cent of the executive producers.[20]

The male monologue does continue to monopolize, determine and often drown out, but women's voices are getting angrier and louder and pushing back.

The male perspective still dominates business

When we began our company, the value of women as customers in all kinds of categories and sectors was just beginning to be discussed. Now of course, the '80 per cent of purchases' figure is flung around as if just saying it will get the cash registers ringing. But you can actually measure which categories take women seriously and which are merely throwing big-sounding figures around.

Businesses still missing the female opportunity

A study of YouTube advertising in 2019 conducted by the Geena Davis Institute on Gender in Media (seejane.org) shows how women tended to be excluded from some categories despite their evident spending power there. There was equal representation of women in consumer packaged goods ads, healthcare ads and, of course, retail ads. However, in automotive, women had only 28 per cent of the screen time, same for business and industrial, and 38 per cent for finance. The speaking time for women also showed similar patterns. Women were speaking for almost half the time in the ads in consumer packaged goods, retail and healthcare, whereas in automotive they had only 24 per cent of the speaking time, 21 per cent in business and industrial and 37 per cent in technology and finance.[21] This, even on one of the newest channels, suggests that old habits really do die hard.

During our time running our company, we have made endless presentations to businesses in categories that have historically been used to develop propositions and communications for men. We have made presentations to car manufacturers about how dissonant what they do is for most women; we have run workshops for telecoms companies explaining how women communicate (and how their companies don't really seem to understand it); we have led off-sites for leadership teams in the financial services space examining how and why they tend to marginalize female customers; we have spoken to political leaders about how policy – and the way it is communicated – can better understand female needs and preferences. At the time, there's always lots of immediate 'in the room' positive murmurings. But when it comes to actually practising what has been preached, the old base settings seem to spring back into play and the murmurings often fade away; while many businesses understand intellectually that women are a valuable audience that they should be making great efforts to reach, there remains, it seems, a resistance to move on from old ideas about how, what and why women buy.

Macho-economics can't accommodate changing female purchase priorities

The 2008 financial crisis had given everyone pause for thought. The 'biggest is best' idea that had driven late-twentieth-century economic thinking suddenly seemed shaky and ill considered. With the onset of austerity across Europe, the hope that a rising tide would carry all ships upward was dramatically and suddenly exposed as false. Big being better was suddenly in question – now bigness was a complicated 'too big to fail' liability that needed bailing out. Globalization too, it appeared, was as significant a threat to stability as it was an opportunity for growth.

Slowly the impacts of the crisis have trickled through to new consumer priorities and behaviour. After years of trolley filling and what women describe in our research as 'mindless' consumption, a new thoughtfulness around purchasing has taken place. A focus on 'savvyness' emerged – women stepping away from unthinkingly buying established big brands, severing old ties and making artful purchases from the newly fashionable discounters, supermarkets and fashion retailers. Middle-class and middle-aged women who previously would not have been seen dead at 'downmarket' outlets now took pride in shopping high and low, finding dexterous deals and proudly describing their smart bargains. Shopping patterns shifted faster than brands could keep up, and many struggled to right themselves (department stores, big estate supermarkets) once the full impacts were felt.

We also began to hear – admittedly at first amongst those who could afford to be picky – an increased 'end-of-gravy-train' interest in sustainability. Now, no marketing director sets out to trash the earth when he or she suggests in a new campaign that women might like a more defined set of eyebrows or a rose-gold phone case. When unchecked, however, the impact of suggesting that endless improvements are required to what are presumably perfectly serviceable eyebrows seems to have been just that. When businesses set out to sell, sell, sell, they did not, initially at least, build into their thinking the consequences for the planet of their ambition. And fast fashion has become the poster boy (or girl) for such unintended fallout. Making clothes has an outsize environmental impact because it requires a lot of water and chemicals, emitting significant amounts of greenhouse gases, and the number of garments purchased each year by the average purchaser has increased by 60 per cent.[22] Where once seasons lasted as long as – well, the length of an actual season, Zara now has twenty-four drops (changes of stock) a year. Items of clothing are now kept for about half as long as they were fifteen years ago, with many of the cheapest items treated literally as throwaway: one wearing and they're in the bin. This then creates a problem at the other end of the purchase cycle, when nearly three-fifths of all clothing produced ends up in incinerators or landfills within three years of being made.

In this era, we began to see women increasingly prioritizing companies' policies around environmental concerns as the impacts of these behaviours rose to the surface – and not just fashion but all kinds of packaged goods. They (85 per cent of them) want brands to show they are conscious of environmental concerns and to build that consciousness into their strategies and models, so they can enjoy buying rather than feel a creeping sense of guilt about it. An online-search-behaviour study of 80 million shoppers in 2019 revealed a 66 per cent increase in searches for sustainable fashion, and predicts that by the end of 2020 10 per cent of all purchases on Lyst – the global fashion search site – will be made with sustainability in mind.[23]

Then there is the impact that the desire for cheaper and faster-changing products has on workers. Social media is working hard here too and has begun to facilitate an open conversation about the treatment of workers in the service of women's appetite for cheap and fast output. Reports of poor working conditions such as the *New York Times* exposé of how fast-fashion online retail brand Fashion Nova treats its (largely female) workers and, most horrifyingly, the Rana Plaza Bangladesh factory fire that killed 1,134 in 2013, have raised women's awareness around the impact their buying habits have on those in the supply chain. It hasn't escaped women's notice that the majority of those impacted by these poor practices are women. Fashion Revolution, an organization that sets out to provide information to consumers about the ways in which different companies address workers' rights, records consumer interest in the issue when it stages a fashion week every year on the anniversary of the Rana Plaza disaster. In 2018 over 3 million people worldwide engaged with the event, taking to social media and generating over 173,000 social posts.[24] In April 2018, the hashtag #whomademy-clothes saw an increase of 35 per cent year on year and a total of 3,838 fashion brands – including retail giants Zara, Massimo Dutti, G-Star Raw and Marks and Spencer – shared information on their workers and suppliers with the hashtag #imadeyourclothes. Fashion Revolution publishes an annual transparency index, revealing the practices of brands who choose to participate and encourages consumers, brands and retailers to take action where they can.

Now 67 per cent of consumers between the ages of sixteen and seventy-five (not sure why the studies always stop at seventy-five, but hey-ho, let's keep moving on) would like fashion brands to tell them where materials used in their products come from; 59 per cent would like to know how their clothes are manufactured; 61 per cent are interested in learning about what fashion brands are doing to minimize their impacts on the environment and workers' human rights. These numbers are particularly high amongst the younger age groups, and while there is a slight affluence bias, it's worth noting that the attitudinal differences between bottom and top earners is only three percentage points.[25]

Companies have been very vocal on these subjects in response, but action is still largely on the periphery – CSR programmes found deep into corporate web pages, or a few lines on modern slavery right down near the 'contact us if you really have to but we won't give you any means of doing so' section.

Where are the women?

Of course, what might help these female priorities get heard and acted upon would be for more women in those businesses to have more influence and more central voices and so help those operations in developing a better understanding. The problem is that progress here has been slow too: only twenty-four of the current Fortune 500 company CEOs are women, and only 5 per cent head those in the FTSE 100.

During this period we began to see, and often encounter, a new leadership style in business. For most of the latter part of the twentieth century – an era often described as one of managerial capitalism – the typical CEO had been a 'company man' who had worked his way up through the ranks on the basis of competence, experience, commitment and skill. He – and it was almost always a he – was no more known to the public than you or I. We often came across him in our days in advertising. He tended to be quite a fatherly sort: very responsible, very dedicated, often quite strict and steely. But, as investors became impatient for growth and that new millennium, new frontiers thinking that we've described took place, this corporate statesman type came to be seen as rather insular and plodding and went out of fashion. He was replaced with a new modern-man breed – the superstar CEO – a man (and again, it was almost always a man) who was blessed with boundless charisma, an enlightened outlook and an unstoppable determination to shake things up to drive the bottom line. As tech and digital became an increasingly central part of business thinking, the influence of Silicon Valley models and personalities began to impact, and to determine what a modern organization should look like, how it should behave and how it should be run. This new breed of CEO came out of that place and was all about Leadership with a capital L: he was there to unleash the energy in the business, inspire the workforce to 'think different', to tear down barriers and to lead company 'transformations' based on new markets, new thinking and new digitally driven opportunities. As part of his magnetism and his drive for growth, the superstar CEO brought with him (to quote the *Harvard Business Review*) 'an almost religious conception of business, exemplified by the appearance of words such as "mission", "vision" and "values" in the corporate lexicon'.

And one of the favourite things that this enlightened, starry CEO liked to do as part of his modernizing and enlightened agenda was – along with his leadership team (which now included Lynda: no longer from 'Personnel' but instead heading up the huge Human Capital Management team) – to examine the vexing questions of 'why women aren't progressing further and faster in business'.

Much has been written, and much has been done, and much has been done with the best of intentions as well as some success, in this space, and you no doubt have read lots of that stuff and probably been on the end of some of those very well-intended initiatives yourself. However, what is completely central to understand here is that throughout this era, the overwhelming focus of the drive has been less about how businesses need to change, or how men need to change in them, but on *how women need to change themselves* in order to succeed. This lean-in view of the world focuses on the challenges that women face in trying to get ahead in business, and, as helpful and instructive and impactful as many of these approaches are, they are, all too often, about how women need to fix themselves. At bottom, many of them come down to a sort of can-do essence; if a woman works hard enough, asserts herself enough, is capable and clear-sighted enough, then she can find a way to thrive at work (and at home). When we interviewed Avivah Wittenberg-Cox for this book (if you don't know her work, look her up. She's written two amazing books on *How Women Mean Business* and *Why Women Mean Business* and is considered one of the world's leading experts on creating gender-balanced organizations). She doesn't mess around:

> All too often, it's about Fixing the Women. That's the approach. It's either about how our own internal obstacles are holding us back, or initiatives that we women can do to broaden understanding within our businesses of what we need. Let's do a female network. Let's coach and mentor women. Let's do classes on how to project confidence. Let's create role-models. Let's all read another book about the Glass This or the Glass That. Work harder, work better, work faster. But it's not about Fixing the Women, it's about Fixing the Organization. Fixing the women puts it all back on them – that can be as much pressure as support.[26]

A willingness to upend the systemic issues that stalled female progress is only nascent at present. So, the initiatives (ugh, initiatives) tend to work at the periphery, where they can't present any risk to business as usual. Female networks? Inspiring speeches about glass ceilings? Yes please. Getting a non-exec woman on the board? Sure. Thinking through how we really treat women in our supply chain? Mmmmm, better not. Or understanding how to configure the working day to accommodate family life? No thanks. Too much. Too disruptive. Too soon.

The squeezed middle in marketing

The picture in marketing and communications businesses reflects a similar reluctance or inability to challenge or change the main game. The usual assumption is that agencies and marketing departments will, by virtue of what they do, be more progressive, and less conservative in their responses to new challenges.

But the response has also been similarly 'initiatives-based'. There has been a huge drive to recruit female creatives through largely female-run initiatives but they have borne little fruit at the top of the creative hierarchy. Cannes introduced a 'special' prize called the Glass Lion to coax the creative community into developing advertising ideas that actively promote gender equality, which is probably helpful but still smacks of exceptionalism. While the number of female marketing directors has reached 33 per cent in the US and 45 per cent in the UK,[27] marketing directors are often squeezed between two crucial roles in the development process that are still overwhelmingly occupied by men: creative directors and CEOs. The men who populate those two roles often get the final say on important brand and communications decisions, so that even when a woman plays a significant role in marketing developments (and by title the *most* significant role), the male lens can often still prevail. This prevalent 'masculine' perspective acts as a kind of handbrake on progress in marketing and can stop real change happening.

We sat in on a pitch process with a client of ours quite recently and the sense of sameness was shocking in a way. If you don't know the pitch process for selecting an advertising agency, the short story is that it's pretty brutal. Agencies are asked to provide (usually gratis) proof that they are the right partner for the client company. The process involves some initial meetings to check everyone likes each other – 'chemistry meetings' or 'tissue meetings' as they're called – and ends with a meeting involving a PowerPoint presentation in which agencies get to show they have understood the client's business and offer up their best guess at a campaign which they believe will make the client's brand even more successful. It's effectively a competition between agencies to win a client's business.

Anyway, sitting through these pitches, more than fifteen years after we had ourselves worked in advertising, revealed to us that in some crucial respects very little has actually changed in agencies' ways of working. It was certainly a more collaborative process, and it obviously featured much less TV and much more digital marketing. However, it was also the case that all the creative directors were men. Almost all the CEOs or senior leaders of the pitches were men. When women were involved on the agency teams, they were most often doing the support roles of account management – the people who organize the team and keep everyone to time – or planners, who are there to 'represent the consumer'. It was striking just how few women were fielded throughout the process, and this was despite the fact that our client is a woman, and her whole team was populated by women, and the consumer audience was women.

'Where are all the women?' our client asked us in the taxi back from one of the pitches. She was actually less bothered by the fact that they were men than about the impact that was having on the creative work they presented, which she felt was out of step with her customers – largely cash-strapped mothers. From her perspective, and from what she had seen so far, choosing an agency with a male dominant team would only lead to ongoing arguments and discussions about things that she needed them just to intuit. She couldn't see them 'getting' her audience in the way another woman might, and the work they produced confirmed her fears. The situation was exacerbated by the fact that our client had spent a year convincing an all-male leadership team back at HQ that the strategy she had given the agency was correct. The agencies had been provided with piles of research around how mothers felt about the brand and what they might respond to in advertising – it was, in fact, a pretty tight brief. However, in the pitches those findings were often ignored or dismissed. In an effort to show their own thinking, rather than use someone else's, the agencies overrode what women had said they wanted in the research documents and produced what *they* thought women would respond to instead. Everything our client had heard in her exhaustive research programme prior to the pitch led her to believe that the ideas they were suggesting would not produce the response she needed to provoke in her audience. In fact, it felt as if the agencies were writing the ads for themselves, not for the cash-strapped mothers she had been hearing from hour upon hour over the last year. She felt thwarted, and particularly frustrated after a long and arduous 'onboarding' of 'the guys' on the leadership team.

It made us wonder at the time what would lead them to believe that they know better than the research when, as individuals, they are so far from the audience (men with salaries in the country's top 1 per cent, living in London vs women from Gateshead with earnings in the bottom 20 per cent)?[28] It wasn't that they were sexists, nor that they were disrespectful. The men in her leadership team and the men in the agencies were trying really, really hard to get the answer right. But they just didn't listen. Not to the women represented in the research and not to our client. In all the meetings, we were sharing the research and they were appearing to listen, but really they were just nodding along politely.

The male glance

Which brings us – on the subject of nodding along politely – to one of our favourite explanatory ideas: the male glance. This was a concept – originally coined by the critic Lili Loofbourow – that sums up this 'listening, but not listening' dynamic that we see playing out in businesses who are 'trying, but not really trying' to understand what women want – either as customers or as employees. It is – like Laura Mulvey's male gaze – a concept that reveals how men look at women, and how they see their work and their worlds. As Loofbourow writes:

> The male glance is the opposite of the male gaze. Rather than linger lovingly on the parts it most wanted to penetrate, it looks, assumes, and moves on. It is, above all else, quick . . . . it feeds a hunger to know without attending, to omnisciently not-attend, to reject without taking the trouble of the analytical labour because our intuition is so searingly accurate it doesn't require it . . . closer to the amateur astronomer than to the true explorer.[29]

In her original essay on the subject, Loofbourow coined the glance to describe the failure by men to take women's stories and interests seriously – she discusses the phenomenon more particularly in the response to work created by women in the arts: so how books and comedies about women become 'chick lit' or 'chick flicks', or how Mark Twain dismissed Jane Austen as incapable of 'high art', or how films made by women are often given short shrift by male reviewers, while equivalent films with equivalent themes but featuring men are pored over and analysed for their greatness. But, more than that, the idea of the glance also describes how subtle and sneaky and between-the-lines those sorts of dismissals often are:

> The Glance is deceptively gentle and ends with a shrug. The danger of the male glance is that it is reasonable. It's not always or necessarily incorrect. But it is dangerous because it looks and thinks it reads. The glance sees little in women-centric stories besides cheap sentiment or its opposite, the terrifically uninteresting compensatory propaganda of 'female strength'.[30]

We imagine the glance was deployed for many years when women were complaining about harassment at work and it only became proper listening when the Me Too movement grabbed men by the ears and made them give the issue their full attention.

When we read Loofbourow's original piece it resonated strongly because we see the 'male glance' in action ALL THE TIME in the way marketing responds to the stories women tell in research. When older women complain they never feature in advertising, the glance responds by saying it would turn off younger women to show them (it wouldn't), or that older women don't spend as much as younger women (they invariably do). When women used to mention the overuse of plastic packaging by supermarkets and how much they worried about the environmental impacts over and over and over again in research, the response from brands was always that there was no viable alternative to it. Yet when David

Attenborough highlighted the impact of plastic on the world's oceans the supermarket brands 'jumped to'.

This idea of the male glance is also very helpful when we come on to look at the way in which marketing has absorbed – or rather glanced at, concluded, and therefore really failed to actually absorb – that women are now conscious of what is being communicated about women, in both the text and the subtext of the way that brands present and behave. And the response from marketing suggests that, in the main, it is not listening to women's stories, or taking them very seriously at all.

Femvertising temporarily takes on the Good Girl

So, remember back to where we were at the end of Part One. The Good Girl model reigning supreme – well, not supreme, obviously; more pleasingly, conveniently, helpfully performing a function that creates lots of lucrative needs and makes lots of sense to the mostly male marketers and mostly male creative teams that used the model.

And use the model they most certainly did, until a challenge to the construct began to appear on the scene: the model that is often cheesily referred to now as 'fempowerment' or 'femvertising'.

This model – in its early iterations at least – offered a new and initially very radical approach to marketing to women: instead of working to stand up and enable the Good Girl, the new model actually sought to show it up for the biased and restrictive narrative that it was. By openly recognizing that the old rules were at best limiting, and at worst punishing, the new approach set out to champion a new way of treating and seeing women: good as they really are, instead of needing to be fixed or other.

The first real example of this new challenger approach was Dove, with their 'Campaign for Real Beauty'. This radical new construct had first appeared in 2004 and took on the ideal of the Good Girl head on. For years, Dove told us, the beauty industry has been telling you that you should be one way, but now we're telling you that it's OK to be the way *you* want to be. Women loved the original campaign – it was mentioned in every single group discussion we conducted for about ten years. Since its success, Unilever has further invested in changing the shape of marketing to women with an industry initiative – the Unstereotype Alliance – that aims to remove harmful gender stereotypes in communications more broadly.

And this initial ground-breaking work certainly did kick a dent in the confidence of those who were used to dropping their latest product formulation into the time-honoured construct of perfection or ideal – flaw identification – science bit – beautiful woman – packshot. And the impact that Dove's campaign had in the market – and the value of the earned media it enjoyed – made many companies think that perhaps women had actually meant it when they said that they were sick to the back teeth of seeing skinny, gorgeous women in communications.

Procter and Gamble should also be given credit for some of their efforts to develop progressive marketing approaches that tried to address the diminishing impacts of the Good Girl world view. The 'Like A Girl' campaign sought to expose the belittling associations the world projects on to girls, and certainly moved the san-pro conversation on from the shame-inducing whispers, codes and euphemisms of the past. Ariel's '#sharetheload' campaign encouraged men in India to do their share of the laundry – and succeeded (to an extent) in rebalancing home chores.

The 'This Girl Can' campaign developed by Sport England is also particularly notable because it features images of women of all ages and all sizes in a completely unmannered way – they're not pretty, they're not young, they're not there to make a diversity statement, they're just there to do sport. And Under Armour – a brand that had for a long time been known for its tough-guy advertising – made progress (and headlines) in 2016 with the 'I Will What I Want' campaign that showed women having the power to be whoever they wanted to be.

Libresse – known as Bodyform in the UK – should also be given a call-out for their '#BloodNormal' campaign that showed – Gasp! Avert your eyes! – REAL blood instead of the blue, in-a-lab substance conventionally used in that cut-away bit in ads where the science bit is offered up. And, more recently, for their 'VivaLaVulva' campaign, which aims to encourage a less hushed and hidden culture around female genitals (a sentence we'd most certainly never have written in 2000).

And finally, last (and, sadly, it is also, as always, least) a special-lifetime-achievement-actor-in-a leading-role award must go to . . . drum roll . . . Helen Mirren for L'Oréal with her tireless work in representing, almost single-handedly, and over a period of at least ten years, the older woman (sfx: deafening roars and rapturous applause as entire marketing industry congratulates itself on remembering to include one of the largest, fastest growing and most affluent demographic groups on earth in just one of literally thousands of campaigns).

By around 2015, 'fempowerment', accompanied by the obligatory hashtag, was absolutely everywhere: from energy companies who'd barely even recognized women up to that point, to san-pro brands who'd for decades spoken about the feminine in hardly heard whispers, to telecoms companies who for years had been slightly mocking of women's conversations as 'chat' or 'gossip' (anyone remember Beattie?), every brand was suddenly rushing to claim its feminist credentials. Again, social media played a big part in what was going on – communications needed to be provocative in order to be shared and what better way to be provocative than to 'catch-on' to this new wave of feminism. It was as if, almost overnight, the advertising industry had suddenly discovered feminism – and was now intent on 'splaining to us all about it.

And now, where we are as we write, it seems as if almost every brand, in almost every sector, has, over the last five years, woven some strand of this sort of activity into their communications. KPMG has told us all about 'the glass ceiling'; Microsoft are empowering girls to #MakeWhatsNextInStem; Verizon has told us to Inspire Her Mind; Toyota is today showing us – in the Super Bowl, no less – how Toni Harris never gave up; Johnnie Walker did Jane Walker; Diet Coke is now telling us that, it's OK, YouBeYou; Gabrielle, by Chanel, lets us know 'that to wear Gabrielle Chanel is to reveal your own intensity, to follow your path and feel radiant and alive'. Across the board, it seems that brands have moved from telling women what they should be and what they're not, and instead are telling us 'you go grrrrrl'. In a move that stunned the industry, the UK Advertising Standards Authority made the surprising decision in 2019 to actually outlaw gender stereotyping. Volkswagen cars and Philadelphia cheese were the first to take a tumble, with much wailing and gnashing of teeth expressed across both the mainstream and marketing press.

And, it is around about this point in time that we first meet Steve at that conference, and he 'splains to us why there is nothing to worry about any more, that marketing had seen the feminist light, that brands are falling over themselves to champion women, that, as CoverGirl now tells us, #GirlsCan.

And to be fair to Steve, through the lens of someone keen to believe that marketing is now fully progressive and true to the modern female perspective, it could appear that this new genre has pushed the Good Girl, finally, into her retirement years. There has been, after all, no shortage of media excitement around the fempowerment movement.

And it would be lovely (although not a very long book) if the story ended there. #MarketingDiscoversFeminism; #TheGood GirlGetsMothballed; #MarketingBecomesAProgressiveForceFor GoodInWomen'sLives; #The End.

But the thing is, that for all Steve's insistence that everything in the garden of marketing is rosy for women, we *know* women don't agree with him. Our data from 2019 show that, despite all the hashtaggery, 66 per cent of women still don't connect with what they are seeing in marketing, and 60 per cent still say they think marketing has an outdated view of women.[31]

However, when marketing seems to have been making best efforts to do the right thing and to earn its feminist stripes, we realize that just saying 'women still don't like most of it' isn't very helpful. What's required instead is a proper assessment of what *precisely* is it in marketing that women still aren't connecting with. So, to offer up that assessment, we undertook a series of projects.

We first conducted a major content analysis (see endnote for methodology) to examine how women were being presented and projected in communications.[32]

We then researched the research that already exists, for which we thank See Jane, the organization responsible for highlighting gender bias in Hollywood started by Geena Davis.[33] See Jane has become interested over the last five years in the measurement of gender bias in marketing as a key contributor to female self-perception and esteem. We have returned to all the research projects that we have conducted over recent years and codified the insights and findings that we think shed most light on the problem and how to solve it. And finally, in partnership with Mindshare, we conducted a study in 2018 that looked at attitudes to marketing and female identity amongst a sample of 14,000 women of all backgrounds, lifestyles and ages across five continents. This study helps us to understand whether the findings from the content analysis suggest that marketing is aligned with where women feel it should be, and whether or not it aligns with how women see themselves.

So, what did all that research reveal?

Well, our first major finding is that . . .

The Good Girl carries on

Beneath the provocative headlines and the eye-catching images of femvertising, the truth is that there is a huge amount of classic and largely unreconstructed brandsplaining out there: brands are still setting out male-pleasing ideals; they're still adopting a 'we know best/better' authority voice; they're still treating women as vacant, dumb and on receive; and they're still 'splaining to women how they should be and how they should behave.

Almost all of the women in the communications we looked at conformed to the Good Girl base setting that we described in the first part of the book. Across the board, women and girls are attractive in a conventional, pleasing, in-the-box way – by which we mean they have shiny hair, clear skin, regular features and are slim. Of the women featured in advertising, 85 per cent could be described as traditionally attractive.[34] Amongst the general public, 80 per cent of women believe that women in advertising are still 'very' thin.[35]

To present a fair and full picture here, we believe it's worth putting those numbers into context. And that context is a pretty distorted one when it comes to women and weight. When we started our business in 2006, the average female model was 20 per cent under her recommended body weight.[36] That idealized super-thin waif ideal, we would say, has been displaced in most mainstream marketing. The introduction of legislation and self-regulation around using women who are dangerously underweight in advertising has pushed the scales up a few kilos. Some impressive example setting and the calling out of the negative impacts of extreme thinness by big brands, spearheaded by Dove, has forced some introspection and changed behaviour in many parts of the beauty and fashion industries. And there has been a culture shift more generally, where women with more generous physiques and larger frames (yes, we do mean the Kardashians) have become more aspirational than the 'pop me in your pocket' model of the past.

But the low, low base from which this 'growth' has come remains merely low. What marketing now presents as 'plus size' in advertising is frequently no bigger than the average woman, and sometimes even smaller than her. Take one particular ad for Boots the Chemist in the UK to get a sense of how distorted the perspective on weight is in marketing. It's a TV commercial where two 'normal' women laugh at a poster that rips off that old Beach Body Ready ad. We're clearly supposed to make note here that they have amazingly sensible and balanced attitudes to their weight. Then, the film cuts to them jumping into the sea in bikinis, apparently, and incredibly, undeterred and unembarrassed by the fact that they are – Shock! Revelation! Denouement! – completely average sized (that's 16 in the UK by the way and between 16 and 18 in the US). The implication here is so distorted: that if you're bigger than a size 8 or 10, then revealing your flesh is so truly remarkable that it's worth making a whole ad about you.

And the prevalence of attractive women is there even in categories not predicated on improving appearance (haircare, skincare, make-up). Women are pretty, even when they're doing the groceries, or serving at a till, or just passing by on the street. In marketing communications, being attractive – in a quite singular way – is set out not just as an aspiration for women but as the norm, which means anything less is an exception – or, worse, a failing. But, as we all know, women who conform to these pretty ideals are in real life the exception rather than the rule, which means we're nearly all failing, nearly all of the time. Which is why 75 per cent of women agree that models in marketing make them feel bad about themselves.[37]

This is not the case in marketing that targets men. Yes, you do get the handsome, square-jawed model advertising aftershave, but in equal measure you find the normal-looking 'bloke', who looks to all intents and purposes like he could have been dragged in off the street. This is a major contribution to the impression women have that their appearance is what matters most about them. Eighteen-to twenty-four-year-olds rate appearance tenth on a list of twenty characteristics that define them, while they say it's number 1 in terms of how society defines them.[38]

Not only are women in advertising very attractive, in many cases they are still sizzlin' hot. In over a quarter of the ads we looked at,[39] women were either pouting, pushing their breasts out, wearing few items of clothing, or looking directly into camera in an alluring manner.

In magazine advertising, this male gaze presentation is much more commonplace and online, as we all know, it is all over the place. The infiltration of pornography into mainstream culture has pushed back the boundaries of how women are portrayed. Now, when brands present women in a sexualized way, the objectifications of the past seem positively tame. Where once they may have been lying on a chaise longue, gazing steamily into camera, now the PrettyLittleThings are aiming their bums at the camera lens in what looks like it's getting perilously close to a money shot. Or they're rolling around on silken sheets on Charlotte Tilbury's web-pages while she, like a boudoir madam, instructs them in the art of creating the 'pillow talk face'. It could be argued that any of the gains made by more diverse presentations of women in other channels are offset entirely by the crushing impact of female presentation in marketing on websites and social media.[40]

Women are still treated as vacant and dumb

The way marketing presents to women suggests it still believes that women are actually pretty dumb. When we ask women what characteristics define them most, they put 'sense of humour' and 'intelligence' as two of the top three – and that's across the world and at every age. In marketing, however, women rarely look like they engage their intellects. Communications present them as happy – in a carefree, birds-tweeting-around-the-crown-of-their-heads kind of way (this compared with the brooding, thoughtful, five o'clock shadowed male presentations). An image that's repeatedly used is the group of women throwing back their heads and laughing together (which, incidentally, we spotted in 20 per cent of ads that feature a woman). Despite being shown as very happy and laughing a lot, in only 3 per cent of ads are women being funny themselves, and in only 3 per cent of ads are they doing something that requires intelligence of some kind. Men speak seven times more than women in advertising.[41] It is hard to be funny and clever in silence. Women in advertising are dumb in all senses of the word.

Women feel irritated when men are featured in household product ads without actually doing any housework. Too often the presentation of men in the narrative mirrors the actually very annoying reality of life: Perfect Mom smiles benignly on while warming the bottles/making the dinner/tidying away the toys/doing the grim detailed bits of housework while Fun Dad tosses the little 'uns in the air. If women were writing that same scene, Perfect Mom's knuckles would be white with frustration and Fun Dad would find himself on the receiving end of the most sullen and resentful stares.

When traditionally female categories decide to target men, the creative approach changes dramatically. Out go mundane illustrations of everyday life: Mom chases toddler around room, voiceover about absorbency, scoops him into her loving arms, cut to contented smiles and packshot, The End. No, when men are in the brand's crosshairs, in comes an aspirational heavy-hitter like John Legend, whom Pampers got on board when they decided to talk directly to Dad (kudos to them for thinking of it). It was literally all singing and dancing. When Tide occupied the Super Bowl, where men would be seeing the advertising, ads went from dreary to award winning. Hilarious, in fact. The creative cupboard gets well and truly raided and the whole arsenal of creativity gets wheeled out in order to capture men's attention: side-splitting jokes, well-known celebrities, incredible locations, brilliant sitcom writers and top-notch production values are all deployed when men are in the audience.

So, where is the funny, clever, creative, imaginative communication for all the funny, clever, creative, imaginative women?

Perfect Mom is still working hard

The decades-old archetype of the Perfect Mom is still very much in play when we look at the channels many first-time mothers use in the early stages of pregnancy: babycare brand websites and YouTube channels.[42] Brands develop these channels as destinations for those seeking advice and help, carefully positioning themselves as authorities in the subject, by providing lots of information about swaddling, napping and burping. Here the imagery featured is almost always of mothers love-drunk on the milky smell of babies' heads, or gazing lovingly into gurgling cots. The promise of maternal bliss gets strongly made here to unwitting women who are yet to experience the challenging reality of being the foundation parent.

Given that three-quarters of women now work outside the home in the UK,[43] and women in the US now hold more jobs than men,[44] it is untenable to assume they can keep holding the baby too. If the gender divide (pay, career success, social status) begins when a baby is conceived, then marketing may still have a lot to answer for as a contributing factor.

Older women are still more or less invisible

If we had a fiver for every time a woman over fifty says to us in research that she never sees herself in advertising, we would have enough for a lifetime's supply of the very best anti-ageing treatments on the market. The reason they feel they don't see themselves in brand communication is that they simply aren't there. Despite the almost single-handed efforts of Helen Mirren, women over fifty feature in only 10 per cent of ads with women in them.[45] (This despite 40 per cent of the UK population being in this age group.[46]) And three-quarters of women over fifty-five agree that they don't see themselves in advertising. Despite the fact this group is the biggest and the fastest-growing consumer audience, and despite their evident 'final salary' pension worth and willingness to spend, the response from marketing departments to the vast opportunity they represent has largely been, in our experience, not even a glance but more a glazed and listless shrug.

The Good Girl is flourishing in unregulated spaces

Finally, and perhaps most regressively, the Good Girl is now out there, refuelled and supercharged by the potent forces at play in the relationship between younger women and the unregulated space of social media. Sitting on sofas in sitting rooms, we hear anxious, almost panicked responses from mothers about how social media is 'getting to my daughter', 'poisoning her mind', 'making her think that how you look is all that's important in life'. We're talking here not just about the user-generated stuff on social media that's created by TikTok-obsessed tweens and scarily disclosing teens. We're talking about the influencer 'brands', and the brands who sponsor them; the Instagram feeds from retail and product brands that feature what seem like an endless feast of perfect pouts and beautiful bodies, going further than television or magazine advertising ever did in presenting women as overtly, now almost aggressively, sexual; the advertising on social media that reads and plays back to women their insecurities and concerns, especially around their appearance. Older Boomer women are especially despairing that everything they fought for as the early feminists seems set back, not furthered, by new technologies. The Good Girl model is still everywhere and it thrives particularly well in the harder-to-regulate, faster-moving places and spaces, where the mercurial nature of the content means that she's almost impossible to catch out, or stamp out.

So that's the first reason women are disconnected from marketing to women. There's still too much of the Good Girl in there. And women don't believe that the Good Girl is good for them any more. But that's not all.

The 'sneaky' stuff

Alongside the more unreconstructed and sometimes even more extreme versions of the traditional Good Girl that are still very much at large are a whole host of practices and constructs that are the very definition of what Rebecca Solnit described as 'the sneaky and hard to point out stuff'. Here brands – largely unconsciously, it has to be said – play out the same old sexist ideas but in a way that's faintly disguised, or subtextual, or implicit rather than explicit. This strand of activity is very strongly present in the analyses that we've conducted: a sort of layer that lies over the Good Girl base settings, giving the nod to modernity and enlightened thinking, but actually continuing – and at worse disguising – the same old tricks and tendencies going on beneath.

Token appearances

There has, without doubt, been some effort in recent years to reflect intersectional ideas in communications and to represent different minorities and ethnicities. The representation of men and women from black, Asian and ethnic minorities doubled between 2016 and 2020, and a 2019 UK study found that there was a black man or woman in 37 per cent of ads,[47] even leading to accusations from right-leaning media that marketing was trying 'too hard' to feature people from ethnic minorities. However, those efforts too often look more like a nod than genuine attempts. Despite the forward movement, 55 per cent of women still say they 'don't feel there is enough racial diversity in advertising',[48] and women of colour notice very acutely when they're always stuck at the end of a line-up of other ethnicities but never given their own starring role. Seeing movement towards the presentation of womanhood in all its diverse glory has been refreshing, but as any woman from an ethnic minority we've spoken to has suggested, when a woman in advertising is from such a minority, her presence is often 'balanced' by white women, or even more often she's lined up amongst a nice, diverse selection of ethnicities. It's rare to see a black woman or girl as the main act in an ad, just representing herself or women, rather than her ethnicity. So, she is there but – perhaps less evident to 55 per cent[49] of the female audience – she's still sidelined in both senses.

Women notice the same phenomenon of tokenism on fashion brand websites. Scroll through the visuals and you'll find a majority of typical slender models, and then – bam! – there she is: the big (by which we mean perfectly normal sized) girl. Scroll again and you could get through five screens before 'another one' pops up – there to amaze you and prove the brand's open-mindedness to such an aberration.

Equally, older women do notice when the only woman over fifty that they ever see in marketing is Helen Mirren. (Sorry, Helen, it's not personal.)

And there's very little that's more token than what has become the standard default setting of modern female marketing – the line-up of diverse-looking women, one blonde, one dark, one ginger, one punky or pixie looking, one skinny but strong, one plus size, one old (or at least older); all laughing, all beautiful, all free to be themselves, #InsertAnyOldBrandHere. This is a construct that we see most regularly in fashion and beauty, but we are also seeing it in retail and in healthcare. We have lost count of the number of times that we have researched a variation of this trope and respondents in research are rightly sceptical: we frequently hear findings that, to cut a long debrief short, amount to: F*** off! #StopTelling-MeWhatIAmOrWhatICanBe. This is lazy tokenism at its worst: you can almost hear the male creative team, sighing wearily at the creative brief, knocking out the easy answer. The glance – 'closer to the amateur astronomer than to the true explorer' – hard at work (but actually not working very hard at all).

This tendency to tokenism also plays out in channel selection. Sneakily, we see brands playing new progressive tunes in the broadcast 'public-face' channels while simultaneously nurturing completely unreconstructed and limiting Good Girl ideals on the quiet in more private ways. Olay produced an advertisement for the wildly expensive and high-profile Super Bowl spot to launch their idea about making space for women in the world, featuring retired astronaut Nicole Stott and TV stars Busy Philipps and Lilly Singh. 'Space is as an idea,' said Madonna Badger about the Olay beauty brand initiative which aims to get more girls into STEM (Science, Technology, Engineering and Maths) – she's chief creative officer (big congrats and welcome to the 12 per cent club[50]). 'It's all about dreaming and new frontiers, the idea that anything can happen. It's always meant that in every country, for everyone. And then we had this idea of "Make Space for Women" have a double meaning, with Busy and Lilly and also an actual retired astronaut.'

So far, so fempowering. But, a couple of clicks away from this advertising is the Olay website on which women are told to 'uncover your eyes not your age' (visual of woman pulling back her eye to smooth wrinkle). To try a touch of Regenerist to make your skin plumper and firmer looking. Or entrust your skin to 'retinol, hydration for smooth and glowing skin'.

Male authority continues – but now wearing a sneaky pseudo-scientific disguise

The good news to report is that the very obvious and overt 'men telling women' voices that used to dominate have largely gone away. Male authority voices are now less the norm and more the exception: men obviously and overtly telling women what they need to do appear in only one-fifth of ads featuring women now. And, again on the upside, the men in white coats – treating women as on-receive patients and co-opting the manly language of science to tell women where they are wrong – have largely vanished from advertising (though not, ironically, from Vanish ads).

But what has taken their place is something that is arguably more sly and insidious – and that's the prevalence of a sort of pseudo-scientific bullshit language. And there's absolutely masses of it out there: 42 per cent of the ads that we looked at featured some kind of pseudo-science. If it helps to illustrate, then here you go . . .

- Lightweight FlexFoam technology pulls wetness away from your skin for Zero Feel protection.
- Stress Response Proteins: Boost skin's moisture retention to improve smoothness.
- Lip Plump-Effect Mustard Sprout Extract – hydrates lips and defines the contours of the lips creating a fuller appearance.
- Supercharged by Matrixyl 3000 Plus, our unique and most concentrated peptide technology to target deep lines and wrinkles.
- 'Kiss-me quick' ingredients – derived from the plant Portulaca, also known as the 'Kiss-me quick' plant, to improve hydration.
- Supreme and global anti-ageing cell power cream.
- Moisturizes deeply* and absorbs in seconds to help restore dry and dull skin.
     * Within stratum corneum.
- Advanced night repair synchronized recovery complex.
- Lasting foundation infused with Hyaluronic acid.
- Total effects 7 in 1 anti-ageing moisturizer and serum duo with Niacinamide.
- Organic Menthol Crystals – create a cool feeling on the lip.

When we ask women in research to read the material on the back of skincare bottles or household cleaning products, the room is often reduced to howls of laughter. 'WTF is a menthol crystal?' is a much more common response than 'I can see now that this product is going to smooth my skin/freshen my clothes/unchap my lips more than another, now I know it's got menthol crystals in it', which is presumably the response that the author is expecting.

Male brands are relatively much more straightforward, practical and level. Some anti-ageing vocabulary is deployed but in general the language tends to focus more on personal comfort than appearance; ingredients are natural and intuitive rather than pseudo-scientific (with willow bark making a strong showing for some reason – must be a guy thing). There is also significantly less overclaim than there is in marketing targeting women:

- Whether you have the face of an angel or the skin of a rhino, Bulldog is on your side.
- Provides all-day relief from 5 signs of skin irritation: burning, redness, dryness, tightness, itchiness.
- This body wash for men helps to hydrate for strong, healthy skin while delivering cooling refreshment and skin comfort.
- How to grow a beard like a boss.
- Key Ingredients: Tea Tree, Lavender, Witch Hazel & Shea Butter.
- 100 per cent Natural Ingredients: Argan Oil (*Argania spinosa*), Jojoba Oil.

What assumptions are being made here with these male brands that aren't made in marketing to women? That men know enough about science to know when they're being bullshitted? That men are sceptical, where women are credulous?

Criticism becomes more implicit than explicit

A further piece of sneakiness that is widespread (and actually slightly encouraged by the femvertising school) is criticism going from explicit to implicit and aggressive to passive-aggressive.

You know the sort of things we mean: products are not 'age-defying', they are 'ageless' or even 'pro-ageing'. Dietary and weight-loss products have become tools for 'wellness' or 'self-care' or 'clean-living'.

Weight Watchers has become WW. Household products are less about terrifyingly germ-filled loos and more about delicious-smelling bathrooms. More sinisterly, your skin doesn't need whitening, it now needs brightening.

Women see what brands are doing when – 'inspired' by the body positivity movement – they twist themselves into knots to translate criticisms of women into more positive sounding 'you can do it' encouragements. They see that the kindness in the words can hide meaner messages, marketing as a wolf in sheep's clothing. This is the all new passive-aggressive approach that the critical eye now adopts. It leaves women with that same uneasy feeling they get when they've had a drink with 'that' friend, who is ostensibly supportive but who says things like, 'I love the fact that you don't care about trends,' and, 'You look so much better with a bit of weight on you.'

They also notice when they're being criticized – even if it's implicit. Here's a small sample of copy we picked out from our product-marketing analysis. Feel free to grab a highlighter and mark up anywhere you spot a critical eye on the customer:

- Fabric Refresher Extra Strength replaces stink with the long-lasting sparkling smell of a freshly cleaned home [regardless of how long it's been since you actually cleaned].
- Removes even body marks, dried-on dirt and grime from the ones you can see clearly to the tougher ones that may be hidden deep in the fabric.
- Lightens dark circles and reduces under-eye puffiness.
- Relieves dark spots, eczema & rashes. Minimizes stretch marks.
- Urban detox mask moisture. Wrinkles visibly reduced.
- NEUTRALIZES ODORS so you can wake up with confidence without changing your routine.

This sample above is pretty representative. So much of what gets said in and around products that target women, points out a flaw in them – explicitly (41 per cent) or implicitly (42 per cent). Rather than feeling lifted up, encouraged, persuaded, 66 per cent of women say they can feel offended by marketing.

Change your mindset and your behaviour – not just your body

Another sneaky trope of this era – and this again is a strong theme in a lot of femvertising – has been a focus on women's behaviours and mindsets rather than their bodies. Following the lean-in school of thinking – where women are told how, with the right positive can-do attitude, they can (must) change the way they think and behave in order to get on – there's now a communications trope that does the same thing. So Pantene 'splains to us that we need to stop apologizing and 'shine strong'; Under Armour tells us we can 'will what we want'; Barbie is #Unapologetic and You Can Be Anything.

Often, when telling women how they need to change their behaviour, what brands say effectively amounts to telling women that they need to be a little bit more like men: so, for skinny, now be buff; for pleasing now be provocative; the Good Girl cliché has become the Rebel Girl cliché. She's told to button up her vulnerabilities, to underplay her sensitivities – strong is the new pretty, be bossy, don't say sorry, lean in, conform to the male stereotype if you want to get along. As Lili Loofbourow would describe it, we've swung from 'Seeing little in women-centric stories besides cheap sentiment' to 'its opposite, the terrifically uninteresting compensatory propaganda of "female strength"'.[51]

Even the most forward-facing initiatives such as gender-neutral fashion ranges feel as though they're saying, 'Look, the female stuff is obviously over, now it's time for us all to be like men.' A cursory investigation of gender-neutral clothing reveals that most of it amounts to versions of what were 'men's' clothes (trousers, sweatshirts, suits) being sold to men and women rather than something truly unisex (where's the rail of unisex skirts?).

Only very, very rarely (Ariel and their 'Share the Load' campaign is the notable exception that proves this awful rule) is it suggested that something other than women might need to change. We are still locked in 'Fix the Women' thinking – and femvertising has done much to perpetuate it. Deborah Cameron, a linguistics professor who has studied how women are constantly told to change the way they speak and write, concluded that

> a woman's place is in the wrong . . . We are told that we say sorry too much, for example, and that this undermines our authority. No one asks if perhaps men don't say sorry enough. Whatever men are doing must be right because they have more power, money and influence. This endless policing of women's language – their voices, their intonation patterns, the words they use, their syntax – is uncomfortably similar to the way our culture polices women's bodily appearance.

And nowhere is this 'fix yourself' sneakiness more obvious than in the media buying of campaigns that claim to 'empower' women: they are, almost without exception, targeted at women or girls. It's a conversation aimed only at women – at best preaching to the converted, at worst underscoring a dynamic that says 'it's all on you'.

There's much to admire in the Always campaign that asked the audience to consider how limiting it is to suggest that when things are done 'like a girl', the implication is that they are doing something worse than a boy would do it – getting rid of that sexist notion is a job worth doing – but are the primary offenders here really young pubescent girls? And should it really be their responsibility to overturn hundreds of years of bias? A beer brand or a gaming brand is much more likely to land the information in and amongst the right audience – the audience that mainly perpetuates the idea and the one who, frankly, created the problem in the first place.

The white-coated scientists have now become shrinks

In the section of the Venn diagram where 'change yourself' and pseudo-science overlap is another trope evident in much of what we see in modern female communications, and most particularly in health and beauty communications: the voice of the therapist. In the good old Good Girl days (though of course she was never old) the male authority figure used to bring white-coated science and the voice of masterly reason to the ditzy, emotional, can't-think-straight, spinning and grinning female audience; now, in the new era, the voice speaks silkily of wellness, vitality and mental health. Products that used to be predicated on the plain-as-the-nose-on-your-face criticism that a woman needed to lose weight remain unchanged except for the packaging: 'be good to yourself' it tells us while selling the same old product with the same old subtext: you need to change.

And nowhere is the Sneaky Shrink tendency more at work than in the booming cosmetic-surgery industry, where brands are 'splaining to women how changing themselves will make them happier. In an ad that runs along exactly the standard parade of women-of-all-shapes-and-sizes-colours-and-creeds lines, MYA, for example, tells us, using the sort of tone you'd use to talk to a ten-year-old, that 'Sherrifa is a feminist who has also had a breast implant (you can do both)', that 'Alice loves her body (most days)' and that 'Aaliyah doesn't think about them any more (since her tubular breast correction)'. The manipulation is so sneaky as to be breathtaking: a surgical procedure to achieve a Good Girl end dressed up as empowerment.

Blue and pink has now become coded

The very obvious pinking and shrinking that used to go on has, we can happily report, now been called out. Recall that Bic 'For Her' biro that provoked all those hilarious responses online:

> Great product! My husband has never allowed me to write as he doesn't want me touching men's pens. However, when I saw this product, I decided to buy it (using my pocket money) and so far it has been fabulous! Once I had learnt to write, the feminine colour and

the grip size (which was more suited to my delicate little hands) has enabled me to vent thoughts about new recipe ideas, sewing . . .

However, while the overt pink-for-her and blue-for-him has more or less been chased out, the highly gendered application of aesthetics – especially in skincare, but it's true for health and beauty more generally – is still going strong. The female brands often look like they belong in that world of girlhoods populated by unicorns and big-eyed narwhals; they're often luminescent, painted in pastels, promising prettiness and sweetness. The male brands, by contrast, belong in a world populated by eligible bachelors who furnish their pads in black leather sofas and own hi-tech sound systems. These products are invariably cool and monochrome in design. They suggest strength, focus and power, while brands that target women favour prettiness, lightness and imagination. It's oppositional sexism – but now in a coded form.

(Note to those who are now sighing that this analysis is becoming trivial, may we refer you to the work of Helen Lewis where she stresses the supreme importance of 'the trivial': 'Sexism is so deeply woven into the words that we use whether it's gendered descriptions such as "shrill" or "bossy" or the fact that it took until the 1970s for women to get an honorific Ms which didn't indicate their marital status. Individually these examples can look trivial but together they quietly shape our entire construction of reality.'[52]

Sexism has a long history of diminishing the feminine interest and perspective as less important and so 'trivial' but it does not follow that it actually is. As Lewis puts it: 'The question of priorities is used against feminists implying that whatever they are currently doing is not the real issue. The real issue is something else.'[53])

The master has become the patron

So, when we look at where we are now and the current state of marketing to women, and examine really deeply and listen really closely to what's going on, the shift that we've seen can be summarized as follows: the brand – designed and set up in the previous era as the master – has, in the twenty-first century, become the patron. It still brandsplains, it still speaks from above, it still talks down, it still sets out what is right and wrong, it still feels its own authority (now with New Added Morality) and is of more interest than its audience, but now, instead of doing all of that in an obvious and explicit way, it has become covert. It no longer sets out to employ a critical eye, or assert a white-coated authority, or belittle with dumbed-down offers or softer, sweeter versions; instead, it uses a sneakier mix of passive aggression, coded language, wisdom bestowed and advice gently given.

The brands we looked at are ostensibly supportive of (and may often, in fact, be sympathizing with) women, but on closer inspection the self-serving nature of what they are saying and what they are doing slips out. They nod along to the dissenting voices that they hear but, instead of really listening, they placate and glance, sticking to the same old base-setting principles but just acting them out in a slightly less aggressive or overt way. They still set out to women what they should be, they still 'splain to them their limitations, and they still offer up the brand as the answer. Women still need to fix themselves, they say; we understand and exist in order to help with that rescue.

This idea that the brand is there to rescue the audience can result in an approach that is almost messianically grand in scope. As part of this project, we examined a number of 'mission statements' of female-targeted brands and were startled by the almighty and from-on-high ways in which they often saw themselves and their role in the world. Here's one from a well-known haircare brand: 'To help women across the globe be strong and shine both inside and out . . . We believe the message of the Pantene video will resonate with women, encouraging them to be more aware of this diminishing behaviour and, in turn, prevent any bias they may be unconsciously creating.'

In this mission statement, women are on the receiving end of 'help' and 'encouragement' from the all-powerful brand. And the particular help they are receiving in this case is to see that their own behaviour is what is causing the sexism they've encountered at work. A dramatic example of the male lens on the problem of gender prejudice in the workplace: fix the women, not the sexism.

Here's another, this time from CoverGirl: 'To inspire people to embrace their unique identities and unapologetically create any version of themselves through makeup. To spark a provocative dialogue that shifts cultural assumptions about when, where, how, and why people wear makeup.'

CoverGirl's mission statement implies the same relationship with its customers as the Pantene example – that the brand has the power and the agency in the relationship – it 'inspires people' and 'sparks dialogue'. It ascribes itself a role in women's lives as muse and provocateur rather than a mere make-up maker.

Or there is the omnipresent L'Oréal beauty and skincare giant that believes in positivity (and listen to the voice of the shrink in this one): 'We all hear that negative voice sometimes. At L'Oréal Paris we believe in the power of affirmations; positive words we repeat to ourselves that can transform self-doubt into self-worth. After all, we've been saying the iconic affirmation "I'm worth it" for almost fifty years.'

It is presumably in that same spirit of powerful positive affirmation that they have named their skincare range (deep breath): Revitalift, Age Perfect Cell Renew, Age Perfect Golden Age, Revitalift Filler Renew; Revitalift Magic Blur Wrinkle Expert; Sculpt School; Infallible Face; No Make-up, Make-up; Age Perfect Make-up; And finally . . . there's Casting Sunkiss Jelly.

The current tendency for brands to present themselves as patrons – there to ride to the rescue, to condescendingly bestow advice or grant the audience its affirmation – is always cringingly evident when they engage in a little light feminism. Here we can find them explaining something to women of which they are already fully apprised because, well, they're women. The male glance doesn't even question whether women think the same way – if it's surprising to men, it must be for women too.

Wrangler, like the cowboy that it is, jumped on the fempower-ment wagon and ran a campaign telling women (over a montage of lots of sexy bum shots, obvs) the glad tidings that 'they were more than just a bum'. And there it is – the brandsplainer – telling women something they already know, as if it is a huge revelation. If anyone thinks that women are no more than a bum, then surely, it is a lascivious male rather than women themselves? Fortunately, women ran Wrangler out of town on social media for such a woefully con-descending effort.

Women are not a special-needs case and Dove is not the answer

Full disclosure: we love Dove and all the work the brand does. We're actually pretty sorry that it can't provide a blueprint for the future because there is so much that's brilliantly helpful in what it communicates both at the grassroots and in the public domain. And there's absolutely no doubt that much of the forward move-ment that has happened in the last decade has happened because Dove changed the game and set the bar – and other brands had to at least glance in response if they were going to keep up.

But Dove, and the other good branded responses to the ways in which women are vocalizing their dissent, don't provide a road for-ward for all brands. In fact, the evidence suggests they are reaching the end of their own road.

First, for their oppositional stance to make sense, most of mar-keting has to be feeding off the Good Girl. And if everyone does that, then everyone will end up on the other side of the fence, opposing something that has ceased to exist.

Secondly, these campaigns that are predicated on standing up for women – even when they do it in the right way, playing the right tunes, acting meaningfully, not making the clumsy errors or reaching for the easy answers – still adopt the role of patron to women. They are operating on women's behalf, and this is no longer what women want. Women don't see themselves as the special-needs case that the patronly stance suggests. Women want the game to change completely. They no longer want to be told or 'splained to – and neither do they have to put up with it. So, changing the game is no longer something that brands can nod along to, or play at, or execute at a superficial level. Eliminating – finally and properly – the brandsplaining relationship and providing women with what they actually want is now a commercial necessity. How to do that will be the subject of the third and final part of the book.

PART THREE

Where We Go Next

Ten Principles for the New Conversation

So, here we are at Part Three: the final part of the book that is all about looking forward.

It's about looking forward because we are now going to present a new vision for marketing to women. We are going to lay out ten principles that together describe a new way for brands to have a new conversation with their female audiences – and eliminate the old brandsplaining practices once and for all.

It's about looking forward because we are now at the stage of the narrative where we can move on from the problem. We know that reading about all the flaws in past and current practice will have been far from easy – particularly when many of the issues that we've been describing are the result of thinking and actions that are not deliberate or even very conscious. In fact, as we've seen and shown, much of the effort has been expended with the very best of intentions. But now, as our silky shrink from Part Two would say, 'You've done the work,' and, on that basis, we are able to move on from problem to solution.

And it's about looking forward because the journey from here really is all upside. As we've shown, the old boxed-in practices of brandsplaining have become restrictive and reductive, not just for female consumers but also for those charged with developing the markets, brands and communications designed to reach them. This part of the book will reveal all the new possibilities and opportunities that open up once those hobbling and hemmed-in settings are released.

Each of the principles is designed to show where and how things need to move on across the ten big themes we've discussed so far: you've read about the brandsplaining base settings, we've described how things have moved on (or not) in the years to date, now we're

How We Got Here: The Origins of Brandsplaining	
1. Gender thinking	Women discussed as 'equal' but different
2. Popular culture	Men control the conversation; women the exception
3. Economic paradigm	Macho biggest is better business
4. The female market	Women emerging in value
5. Organizational culture	Woman valuable but secondary
6. Marketing authorship	Marketing man in charge
7. The marketing lens	Male lens
8. The dominant concept in marketing	The Good Girl – made perfect
9. Marketing constructs	Perfectionist narratives: And the award goes to . . . men The real thing is male Stick to male-pleasing ideas Adopt a critical eye Denial narratives Treat women as vacent and dumb Male authority voices Women grateful to receive
10. Attitude to masculinity	Masculinity is primary

Where We Are Now: The New (But Not So Improved) Version	Where We Go Next: Ten Principles for a New Conversation
Women call out toxic femininity	Accept that women now please themselves
Women's voices strengthened by social media	Show what was the exception as the rule
Globalization (not good for all)	Put an end to macho-economics
Businesses still missing the opportunity	Catch up with the expert
Fix the women	Mend it for everyone
Female marketing directors stuck in the middle	Prepare for the primacy of female-made brands
Male glance	Stop looking – and start learning
The Good Girl continues – camouflaged by femvertising	Forget ideals – present a grounded and granular understanding
The 'sneaky' stuff: Token appearances Male authority in disguise Implicit criticism Change your mindset and behaviour Authority voices are now shrinks Pink and blue in code Women not a special-needs case	Be constructive not critical: Treat positive subjects, positively Assume women mean it when they say it needs fixing The least you can do is be clear and funny Be straightforward Treat gender as performance
Masculine is still the aspiration	Acknowledge sexism goes both ways

going to show how, in each area, change needs to happen and what that change looks like. For those of you who like to see what's coming next, the table on the previous pages shows a preview of the ten principles, showing how they represent a move onwards from the key themes that were discussed in Parts One and Two.

Principle 1: Accept that women now please themselves

This first principle is based on the most fundamental shift in the female perspective that we have observed: the belief that living a satisfying, fulfilled life no longer relies on pleasing men.

Under the old model, the whole of female life is shaped as a bell-curve: at the first stage a slow build towards becoming a projection of femininity that men will find appealing enough to want, then mother-hood as the high point of achievement (and thus the more perfect the better), followed by the third downward stage represented as an inev-itable and fairly immediate decline into obscurity and irrelevance once child-bearing responsibilities have been delivered. Movement up the curve is determined more by how a woman looks more than by who she is. And her advance or failure is determined by how much (or how little) she impresses men and meets their ideals. And, just to add insult to injury (and those words really are apposite, these practices are both insulting and injurious), progress along the bell-curve is accompanied by a continual background narrative whispering in her ear that the efforts being made towards achieving those ideals are not enough: that more is needed, that perfection should be worked towards, that just another little fix can get her closer.

As we've discussed, in the fifteen years we've been in business there's been a heightened and widespread recognition that those Good Girl boxes are immensely restrictive for women, and are, in fact, the underlying reason why we continue to live in a world where it is men who are almost always in charge almost all of the time – and women are cast into a secondary position. Fourth-wave feminism – in fact, all the waves of feminism – has been about challenging all of that, and we are now in an era where new projections of women, projections that aren't the result of having to be pleasing to men, can come to the fore.

Instead of working to portray ideals that suit men, marketing should now be working to portray women as they really are. So, take away the male projections, stop looking from the male vantage point, eliminate the male gaze, lose the man-made bell-curve construct and hear from women as they are and want to be.

Once all those projections are stripped away it's clear that the female lives and aspirations that women voice have changed and are changing. Because, while the male-pleasing ideals we've described have – subject to a slight move from the explicit to the implicit – remained broadly constant over time, throughout the twenty-first century, and at every life stage, women's lives and perspectives have changed significantly. Fortunately for us, as a result of our research practice we've had ringside seats to view those changes; we've seen and heard at first hand how women's lives are altering, and how they look once the prism of male ideals is removed.

Education, education, education

The first shift that has taken place is in female education and attainment. These changes are moving dramatically and rapidly, and reshaping the bell-curve with their impacts. More or less across the board, girls are now outperforming boys in their educational achievements. In England, for example, girls do better than boys in all subjects by the end of primary school, with SATS scores showing that 70 per cent of girls reach the expected standards in maths, reading and writing compared with 60 per cent for boys.[1] At GCSE, more than 25 per cent of entries by girls received the top grade of A or 7, compared with 18.6 per cent for boys.[2] And while nearly three-quarters of grades for girls were a pass at level 4 or above, only two-thirds of boys achieved the same.[3] At A level, female students score more A and A* grades than boys in every subject other than maths, further maths and chemistry.[4]

And, in case you're wondering about girls and STEM as the

exception to these rules, there's amazing progress here too: in 2019, the number of girls taking science A-levels overtook boys for the first time ever.[5]

At higher-education level, the results are even more dramatic. Participation levels for young women in the UK are now at 56.6 per cent (compared with 44.1 per cent for men), up from 46.5 per cent in 2007.[6] By 2025, the Organisation for Economic Co-operation and Development (OECD) forecast that the percentage of female students in higher education in the UK will have risen to 71 per cent.[7]

The same study reports that the reversal of gender inequality at higher education levels is true across all the OECD countries. Until the mid-1990s, more men than women received higher education and obtained degrees – 1.2 men for every woman, in fact. By 2025, their forecasts predict that picture to have been completely reversed: their estimates suggest 1.4 female students for every male. In some countries (Austria, Canada, Iceland, Norway, the UK) the model predicts there could be almost twice as many female students as male.

The huge and rapid leaps in female education play out – albeit in a much patchier way – globally. While there is still a huge distance to go in terms of both the participation and the quality of education for girls, there has been marked and massive recent progress.

All these very significant and very rapid shifts in female educational attainment chip away at the notions of male dependence that power a bell-curve view of female life. With education come agency and confidence, and with agency and confidence come a preparedness and an ability to please yourself.

Single women don't need (or want) a man

Alongside – and accelerated by – these shifts in education and shifts in attitudes to gender, we're also seeing a further challenge to bell-curve thinking in the form of shifting attitudes to single life or a life free of male partnership. In 2009 the proportion of women who are married in the States dropped below 50 per cent for the first time.[8] When and if women do marry, they are marrying at a later stage in life – in 2017, the average age for women in the UK to marry passed thirty-five for the first time.[9] This is a marked generational shift when you consider that in the 1970s the average age that women married was just twenty-two. In the rest of Europe, the mean age at first marriage is higher than thirty in Germany, France, Spain and many more of the region's more developed economies.[10] Today in the US only 20 per cent of Americans are married by the age of twenty-nine, compared to nearly 60 per cent in 1960.[11]

And the marriage rate – the number of eligible people who marry – is also down. In the UK it is at its lowest rate since matrimony records began in 1862. The rate for women is now just 19.8 marriages per 1,000 unmarried women – less than a third of the level in 1972 when marriage was at the height of its popularity.[12] In Japan, a nation with one of the most dramatically falling marriage rates, citizens have begun to abandon not just marriage but heterosexual sex. It's a phenomenon they describe as *sekkusu shinai shokogun*, which means (just for the few of you who don't speak fluent Japanese) 'celibacy syndrome'. One study found that almost 60 per cent of unmarried Japanese women aged between eighteen and thirty-four were not in any form of romantic relationship.[13] And according to the Japanese magazine *Joshi Spa!*, which polled more than 37,000 people for their thoughts on marriage, 33.5 per cent thought it was pointless.[14] In Italy, the marriage rate has dropped from 7.7 per 1,000 inhabitants in 1960 to just 3.2; in Germany it's now 4.6, down from 9.5.[15]

And women are waiting longer to have kids too. In 2017, for the first time, more women in the UK became pregnant over the age of thirty than in their twenties. The average age for women to have their first baby is now 28.9.[16] Many are deciding to have no, or fewer, children – the birth rate is dropping fast in all developing countries and, in the US, is at its lowest rate in over thirty years.[17]

All of which heralds and reflects a marked new shift in female independence – and with it a freeing up of the need to please, oblige, agree and conform that is so inherent in the old sexist mores. The findings from the study we conducted revealed very clearly that female aspirations were about independence from someone else's ideals: in fact, the highest aspiration of all centred on the rejection of other people's projections – 'to be comfortable in my own skin' was the statement that topped the list, with a 68 per cent agreement level. 'To be financially independent' had the next highest level of agreement at 62 per cent, and 'To be able to make my own decisions in life' came in at 60 per cent, followed by 'To not be concerned by what other people think about me' at 51 per cent.[18]

Equally revealing were the statements about aspiration that had the lowest agreement levels: only 11 per cent agreed with the statement 'To be able to give up my job if I have children'; only 16 per cent wanted 'To be admired for how good I look' and only 23 per cent went along with 'To find a partner who can look after me'. This rejection of having to 'appear' in order to please men was also strong in the data. One of the lowest scoring statements, at 40 per cent, was agreement with the notion 'To get on in life you must behave the way that men prefer', while one of the highest scoring statements at 76 per cent was 'I would rather be praised for my mind than my looks'.[19]

Mothers don't feel the need to be perfect

When we first started out, the 'having it all' ideal was at both the heart and the height of the bell-curve. A woman's life, focusing on hopes of motherhood as the most notable purpose of early adulthood, and idealizing motherhood as the most fulfilling part of life, with the post-maternal years cast as a depressing decline, still shaped expectations and aspirations.

With this came tremendous pressure to conform to an ideal of perfect motherhood, both for mothers who were working outside the home and for those who weren't. Mothers who didn't work outside the home, especially those who had school-age children, gave lots of time and mind space to being an almost professional-level parent, even if that couldn't always be achieved. When it couldn't be achieved they said they felt as if it was a job they were failing in – words like 'terrible mother', 'letting my children down', 'not doing my job properly' fell easily out of their mouths.

Conversations with mothers who did work outside the home were marked by the language of coping, struggling and an overwhelming sense of underachieving and compromise in their role. They didn't have the time and mind space to give to the ideal, and the load at home had still not left their maternal plates. One woman described the constant raising of the ideals and expectations as 'like a glass of water being filled by a tap that never goes off. The water goes up and up but the filling never stops and there's nothing draining out. In the end, it all ends up just spilling over.'

The additive effect was hugely burdensome. Both working and non-working mothers felt compelled to present a swan-like calmness to the outside world, but our sessions with them sometimes ended in despairing tears and a mix of self-flagellation and bitter recriminations about the unfairness of it all. Almost three-quarters of working mothers said they were struggling with wellbeing, and 40 per cent described themselves as hanging by a thread. They were doing over three hours more unpaid work in the home than their male counterparts and only 16 per cent of them said they were satisfied with life overall.[20]

Finally, the lid blew off the pressure cooker, something broke in women, and in what feels like some kind of subconscious collective agreement, women decided that trying to be perfect was hurting everyone, themselves most of all. Me Too advanced the cause by highlighting the institutional barriers and endemic inequities that no amount of leaning-in could shift. When promoting her book *Becoming*, Michelle Obama seemed to sum up what millions were thinking but hadn't quite dared express. 'I tell women that whole "you can have it all" – nope, not at the same time; it's a lie. It's not always enough to lean in, because that shit doesn't work all the time.'[21]

Calling out the silent work

At the same time as seeing cracks appear in the Perfect Mom conventions, we are now also beginning to see a brilliant new focus in the managing of work and home discourse: the revolutionary idea that men need to do some fixing too, not just in the workplace, but, perhaps more profoundly, in the home space. For many years, feminists have been talking about the burden that unpaid work puts on women, and the inequality of domestic labour: the 'second shift' as it was described by Arlie Hochschild back in the 1970s second wave of feminism. Yet, despite the years that have followed, and the increasing responsibilities that women have taken on at work during those years, the promise of egalitarian households has remained largely elusive.

Many men do much more housework and childcare than they did in the 1970s. In the UK Office for National Statistics' 2016 Time Use Survey, British men claimed to do eighteen hours a week of domestic labour, which certainly compares well to the one hour and twenty minutes of a man in 1971. Yet these eighteen hours are much less impressive when looked at alongside the thirty-six hours a week that female Britons devote to household chores. And British men give themselves five more hours of leisure time than women do.[22]

And this picture is pretty much tru[...] the States, men contribute seven hou[...] teen; Australian men five hours to women's fifteen; in Italy it's apparently a staggering twenty-four and a half hours a week to men's three and a half (*vergogna per voi uomini*) and in Portugal it's down to a paltry three hours for men compared to women putting in twenty-two. Even in good old Sweden, where they always do the right thing when it comes to gender, women are doing forty-five minutes extra each day.[23] Those figures don't take into account all the many extra hours that women are devoting to what author Sally Howard calls 'silent work': 'the mental load of assuming the responsibility for running a home: chivvying unwilling partners; or the emotional labour of keeping everyone happy and maintaining extended family relationships'.[24]

In our research, we've regularly heard women 'moaning' about the lopsided nature of the domestic load, with lots of amusing anecdotes about the stuff that men do or don't do, and many wry observations around the syndrome where male domestic work garners disproportionate praise. One woman told us how her mother-in-law gasped 'Isn't he marvellous?' when her son mashed up a few potatoes; another how her partner proudly thinks he's done wonders by putting the mug next to, but never in, the dishwasher. During the 2020 pandemic lockdown, many women reported how – despite both parents being at home – the majority of the domestic burden continued to fall on their shoulders. Research carried out by economists from the universities of Cambridge, Oxford and Zurich found that both employed and unemployed mothers were typically spending around six hours providing childcare and home schooling every working day. By contrast, the average father at home was only spending a little over four hours on childcare and home schooling each working day, regardless of his employment status. 'Whatever situation you have, on average it's the woman doing more, and it's not because she's working less,' said Dr Christopher Rauh, an economist at Cambridge University and one of the authors of the study.[25]

However, what has moved forward is an awareness and understanding of the nature and impact of this inequality. Recently, a book called *Fair Play* became a *New York Times* best seller. Written by lawyer Eve Rodsky, it's an account of the domestic gender imbalance and its destructive effects on female progress and happy relationships and lives: 'I fundamentally believe this is the last frontier of feminism that nobody talks about. I had someone say to me "yes, I was part of #MeToo movement – I was sexually harassed – but you know what's actually even more detrimental to my career? The way my husband deals with housework."'[26]

She began the book by compiling a gargantuan list of all the responsibilities, decisions and daily admin that female lives entail – 'Sh*t I do' – and followed it up by interviewing dozens of academics and couples to understand how this incredible imbalance in the domestic agenda occurred. She puts it down to the fact that women become the default – or, as she calls it, the 'she-fault' – for every child, parent or household task. Men might do some tasks as instructed, but they still don't consider it their responsibility to pick up the reins: even the most enlightened still need prompting, coaching, instructing and praising.

Sally Howard's book *The Home Stretch* has also pulled into the light this aspect of inequality and its huge impacts. Interestingly both Howard and Rodsky begin their narratives with similar anecdotes: both tell how they felt they were successful working women, considered the world an equal place, had never felt the impacts of sexism or inequality, thought that they were married to enlightened partners who also thought of themselves as enlightened, both felt they'd cracked this whole having-it-all thing, until they had a baby. From that moment, an imbalance opened up: 'the parent labour trap where economic and structural forces discipline many of us, however much we struggle or hope to avoid it, into traditional gendered roles once kids arrive on the scene'.[27]

Curiously, to date, we've seen few brands participate, or seek to support their customers, in this interesting space. They have been much more comfortable in initiatives to support girls' education, or girls' confidence, or positive beauty, but strangely quiet or otherwise occupied when it comes to picking up the mop and getting stuck into helping clean up the messy realities of an unequal domestic load.

Women over fifty aren't hiding any more

And then to the last male-prescribed archetype – women over fifty – who have, since the very earliest of marketing's days, been treated as one of the least significant and least interesting audiences in the world.

In research discussion after research discussion we hear women talk about how the older they get, the more invisible they feel they become. In meeting after meeting we hear clients either ignore or discount older women as an audience in favour of brighter, younger things. And in marketing portrayal after marketing portrayal we see this audience being misunderstood, misrepresented and, all too often, missing completely.

In a recent research discussion, we asked women to describe how they felt they were seen and depicted by advertisers – and how those descriptors matched (or not) their own view of themselves. Respondents were all too familiar with the reductive ways in which they were depicted and diminished, and so responses came easily. First up, and most familiar, was the frail old lady – you've probably seen her (or rather you've probably overlooked her) yourself. You'll find her at the back of most supplements: faint, grey and enfeebled, probably about sixty but cast to look and behave as if she is a bewildered centenarian.

Next, is her more sprightly friend, the comedy granny, who appears looking slightly batty, sometimes dressed in mismatched or out-of-time clothes, a faint 'I-don't-know-what's-going-on' look in her eyes. She's usually there as a prop to throw into relief the youthful virtues of others in the communication – the loving warm family who have her along on special occasions; the successful tech savvy son who has provided her with technology so that she can see him even if she can't be with him; even (and yes, Dolce and Gabbana, we know your game) as novelty 'characters' surrounded by decades-younger models in a fashion shoot. She is never there in her own right or as the protagonist in her own script: her role is as a token, the exception that proves the rule, the joke in the background, the show of authorial inclusivity and enlightenment.

Third up is the unfeasibly and paradoxically young and beautiful older woman: a woman who is officially in the older age bracket but, in reality, could be mistaken for someone almost half her age. Interestingly, this woman is often shown looking wistful, with a tinge of look-back-in-sadness in her expression, longer hair blowing in the wind – almost as if the photographer, with his male lens firmly attached, is conveying loss, how much she misses the better days of her youth and regrets their passing.

And then last, and in a very real sense completely and utterly least, is the invisible woman: the startling absence of older women in communications, not included simply because they are not considered relevant, or, more likely, just not considered at all. The feeling of invisibility that women report in our groups is not imagined: all too often older women are conspicuous by their absence, overlooked and effectively 'disappeared' as they age.

Throughout all these depictions and presentations and non-depictions and non-presentations, the themes are the same: older women are lesser, limited, lost, regretful, on the sidelines and away from the main scene and stream. The lens through which they are seen brings the double whammy of marketing's male gaze and youth fixation, and the multiplying effect of both is belittling. The youthful lens interprets its own state as being dominant and the high point of life; through that prism the older age state is seen and shown as a lessening – a lessening of power, of relevance, of worth and of ability. Yet this erosion simply does not happen in the same way with men, who, in older age, are typically shown as silver foxes or wise leaders, their grey hair a mark of wisdom, their eyes twinkling with 'still got it' charm and appeal.

To be fair and to give some benefit to all this doubt, there was a time, not so long ago, when these 'gentle' depictions of the older female audience were more relevant and appropriate than they are now. Up until the early years of the twenty-first century, the older female audience represented those who had been born between 1912 and 1945 – the cohort that *Time* magazine has described as 'The Silents'. This generation – brought up in the world wars and their aftermaths – were distinctly traditional, raised to comply and to conform. Their formative years were frequently characterized by rationing, by separation, by austerity and by the head-down hard work that was required to move beyond wartime destruction. They were raised on the wartime need to bestow huge respect on the establishment and to follow social orthodoxies, and were considered by many to be the first generation in history who were more cautious and conformist than their parents. Jobs, political allegiances, marriage, social class were all signed up to early in life and, generally, were for life: people knew their place and stuck to it with compliance and without complaint. A blog post from an

American woman of that generation describing her formative life influences sums up the outlook brilliantly:

> My generation, born between 1928 and 1945, was identified as Silent when many of us were still too young to protest, even if we had been inclined to speak up. As early as 1951, TIME Magazine pronounced us cautious, risk-averse, and conforming. The reason – or excuse – for these unexciting characteristics was that having spent our childhood during the Great Depression and the Second World War, we learned early in life to share tea bags, put on grey flannel suits, and inquire about pension plans at our first job interview. We grew up in the shadow of our heroic elders, the Greatest Generation who won World War II, only to find ourselves, before very long, in the deeper shade of our enormous children – the Boomers.
>
> Blog Post. Clarissa Atkinson. Age 77[28]

For women of that silent generation, this tendency to take a passive, cautious, compliant role was much stronger than for men: choices were dramatically limited and the pressure to be, and behave as, a Good Girl was great. Women were living lives that were largely dependent on men – their primary roles were domestic and their choices predetermined by society, family standing and social norms. Working-class women worked outside the home – but almost invariably in the low-paid, low-value '5C' roles that depended on male patronage (no, that's not C-Suite roles, Steve, it's C standing for Cleaning, Catering, Clerical work, Cashiering and Childcare). Middle-class women tended to work only until they were married – and then in roles like teaching, nursing and secretarial jobs that were designed to display and to hone their Good Girl skills. It was a largely pre-feminist rulebook world where women were presented with few choices and had limited inclinations or opportunity to do other than conform to male ideals.

This silent generation of women was also, unsurprisingly, rulebound and biddable consumers. Raised in scarcity economies, they adopted a 'make do and mend' outlook that was the mirror opposite of the rampant consumerism of later generations. Spending on non-essentials was limited by a responsibility-before-pleasure outlook; the authority of 'the big brands' was unquestioned in the same way that authority was unquestioned generally. The 'we-know-best' approaches of the brandsplainer aligned with the 'we-know-best' approaches by the establishment and culture as a whole. In this context, it is perhaps understandable that marketing's habit of seeing older women, if it sees them at all, as mild and inconsequential was formed.

So, with the benefit of that doubt now given, let's turn to the reality of who and how older women actually are, and how dramatically different that is from the depictions that continue to inform the basis of standard marketing approaches. The first – and most central – point to understand is that those in this age cohort are pretty much the opposite of the 'Silents' who parented them: born in the years between 1945 and 1964, they are the Boomer generation and, unlike their parents, who grew up with the belief that their role was to conform to the world, this generation grew up with the belief that their role was to change it. As *Time* magazine described them in 1967 – when the term 'Boomer' first became a thing:

> This generation looms larger than all the exponential promises of science and technology; it will soon be the generation in charge. If the statistics imply change, then the credentials of the younger generation guarantee it. Never have the young been so assertive or so articulate, so well-educated or so worldly. They are a highly independent breed . . . not just a new generation but a new kind of generation.[29]

And change the world was exactly what they did: setting out to question and upend the conventions and conformity of their parents' generation, this generation set out to remake themselves and remake the world. Fuelled by the advances of science, technology and the boom-time era of global regrowth and state support, they questioned the confines of almost everything: civil rights, sexual freedoms, war and anti-war, drug experimentation, the economic model, even travel beyond the confines of the earth.

And with all of that came the women's movement and the questioning of conventional roles and restrictions: no longer living in a 'know your place' world, women set about making themselves, often directly rejecting the conventions and conformity of their parents. Participation in higher education and in the workplace reached unprecedented levels; parenting was redefined as the stiff 'hurry up and grow up' attitude of the previous generation was replaced by a Doctor Spock-influenced world where affection and the recognition of children's needs were encouraged. Consumerism – in the way that we have now come to understand it – came into being as affluence, choice, supply, demand and competition grew. The seeds of destruction were being sown for the idea that this female generation was a passive group ready and willing to be 'splained.

And now, with this cohort of women at retirement age, living a post-work and post-family life, we see this non-compliant, self-determined tendency coming fully into its own. These women were the first feminists, the first teenagers, the first consumers, the first professional parents, the first to forge their way in the modern workplace, the first to have their own incomes . . . and now, they are setting about being the first generation of women who see 'retirement' as an invitation to do the very opposite. Across the board and across our different research studies we see this generation of women tearing up the rules and living lives that are the very opposite of the mild and receding depictions of most marketing. As *The Economist* describes it:

Baby-boomers have spent their lives making noise and demanding attention. They are not going to stop now. They will be the biggest and richest group of pensioners in history. They will also be the longest-lived: many will spend more time in retirement than they did working. The baby-boomers have changed everything they have touched since their teenage years, leaving behind them a trail of inventions, from pop culture to two-career families. Retirement is next on the list.[30]

In research, this group tell us that these later years of their lives are the opposite of recessive, quiet and reduced: they are, to use their words, a time of 'blossoming', 'flowering', 'coming into my own', 'finding myself', a stage where I can be 'just me not trying to please anyone else or be anyone else'. Far from being a time of ebbing presence or diminishing agency, these years are, for many women, the first opportunity for 'me-time': free of the responsibilities of looking after others, working at home and out of it, holding in their heads all the cares and needs of other people, this stage of life feels like a time of enlightenment. They describe a sense of freedom that comes from leaving behind the self-consciousness of their younger years, and with them the warping impacts of having to please and conform. They have a much stronger, more reliable sense of who they are as people and what makes them happy – and depend much less on the validation of others (particularly men). It is as if they are, at last, free from having to fit themselves into the man-pleasing boxes of the Good Girl, and can finally step out to blossom into their true selves for the first time.

And with this sense of enlightenment, growth and self-determinism comes a willingness to speak out and stand up. Far from the timid and faint depictions of marketing, members of this audience are, in fact, more sure and more certain and willing to make themselves – and make themselves heard – than many of their younger counterparts. In our study, 85 per cent of this age cohort said it's now more acceptable for women to be outspoken and bold, and qualitatively we regularly hear a rebellious willingness to 'run (their) stick along the public railings', particularly on behalf of other women. Eighty-nine per cent agree that women shouldn't be pressurized to get married and have children; 78 per cent say it's good that traditional family roles evolve and modernize.

And the priorities and values of this age cohort also change in other equally interesting – and under-acknowledged – ways. The value of enjoying life slowly comes more to the fore: the pleasure in time taken and in the moment enjoyed are stronger at this life stage than at any other. Whole health becomes more important – both mental and physical and the connections between the two. The natural world comes more to the fore – particularly the beauty in nature and the calming and connecting effects of being outside. Interests and learning come back into focus: creativity, often repressed in the family-life stage, returns and self-improvement becomes an important part of making the most of yourself and your time. Lynda Gratton, co-author of *The New Long Life*, talks about the growing importance of 'Intangible Assets' at this stage of life – the need to nurture, alongside the tangible assets of pensions, property and savings, the intangible assets needed to enjoy life to the full: vitality, productivity, novel-action taking, exploration and experimentation. Altruism and activism also become more important: after years of looking after the close family, a focus on the wider community and contribution is now achievable.[31]

Yet virtually none of this outlook or occupation comes across in the way that marketing treats this audience. Instead of the sure-footed, self-determined approach that underscores how the audience see themselves, marketing sees them as frail and needy. Instead of the buoyant, blossoming way in which the audience take on what life has to offer, marketing talks to them in tones that are sympathetic and low key. Instead of recognizing the rich, colourful, opening up of life at this stage, marketing continues to view this age as beige, boring and reduced.

This complete mismatch between how the audience see themselves and how marketing sees them represents not just a massive failure – what is marketing about if it is not about understanding the audience? – but also a massive missed opportunity. The population of over sixty-fives in the UK was described by NESTA as 'the fastest and largest growing demographic group ever recorded'. In 1998, one in six people in the UK was over sixty-five years (15.9 per cent of the population); by 2018 it was one in five (18.3 per cent); and by 2038, it is projected to be one in four people in the population (24.2 per cent). By contrast, the percentage of adults aged sixteen to sixty-four is in sharp decline: in 1998 it was 63.6 per cent of the population; by 2038, it's projected to be just 58.4 per cent.[32]

In the US, the pattern is very similar. Today, just over 34 per cent of the population is over fifty, and their numbers are rising rapidly with the ageing of the Boomer generation. The oldest baby boomers hit age fifty in the mid-1990s, nearly doubling the number of people in the pre-retirement age group of fifty to sixty-four from 32.5 million in 1990 to 58.8 million in 2010. Population growth amongst sixty-five- to seventy-four-year-olds is set to soar: their numbers are projected to climb from 21.7 million in 2010 to 32.8 million in 2020 and then to 38.6 million in 2030. And because, as in the UK, older age groups will be growing more rapidly than younger age groups, their share of the overall population will also increase sharply. Today, one in seven people in the US is at least age sixty-five; by 2030, that share will be one in five. At the same time, one in sixteen persons is now aged at least seventy-five; by 2040, the share will be one in eight.[33]

And, to date at least, this audience represents a hugely affluent group, buoyed up by final salary pensions and booming property prices. As the Institute of Fiscal Studies described it:

> Those aged over 65 are more numerous and prosperous than ever before. Moreover, their numbers are set to swell as the century progresses. The affluent over 65s are therefore likely to be the growth market of this century, and the nation's future economic performance may well hinge on the ability of producers to meet the needs of this burgeoning market.[34]

But, despite all of this, the older female audience continues to be overlooked and under-understood. The double whammy of the youthful lens and the male lens is, it seems, too entrenched and too inflexible to see what is happening right in front of its very eyes: a vital and valuable target audience, completely altered from the generation that preceded it, ripe with unmet and unrecognized needs, and full of radical promise.

So, that's principle number one – accept that women now please themselves – and it's first for a reason: it's the very foundation upon which new marketing approaches have to be built. No more women-according-to-men. No more laying out of male-pleasing ideals. No more bell-curve view of the shape of female life. Strike from the record the Good Girl settings. Look and listen to what women really are and are becoming. Accept that women now please themselves. And, when you do, you'll see a present and a future that's so much richer, more brilliant, more radical, more uplifting, more buoyant, more interesting and more forward-looking that you'll be only too happy to leave those reductive, boxed-in, on-repeat, two-dimensional stereotypes in the past where they now belong.

Principle 2: Show what was the exception as the rule

We have heard how the base settings of marketing were predicated on women being on the receiving end of a male-dominated culture and media. And we've heard how, over the last fifteen years, social media has created a channel that means women's voices can't be muted or edited or boxed off as secondary. So now we're at a place where those female voices, and particularly the ones that challenge the old constructs, really get heard. We can reject both the tedium and the torture of the Good Girl limitations – and embrace instead a fully updated and rebooted version of womanhood that is now accessible for all to experience. Because, interspersed between *Love Island* (grrr) and the pretty-as-a-picture Nick tweens, there are female role models emerging that don't feel like they were cooked up in a lab full of leering or demanding men. What may be less pleasing, of course, is that lots of what these women convey, and the way in which they convey it, does not make any attempt at amelioration. The female voices making themselves heard now – through social media and in new creative content (often created by women) – are often the voices of 'bloody difficult' women.

Across the board, authentic female stories and voices now traverse all platforms and channels as producers and commissioners finally acknowledge their appeal. And, unmediated by male interference, women are projecting a version of femininity that is on their own terms, not men's.

High-penetration subscription streaming services such as Netflix, which don't rely on the conservative impulses of advertisers or the need to create only mass-market and mainstream content, are providing a platform for female characters who don't stick to the rules of male ideals. These characters aren't sitting willingly in second place but always take the lead – *Orange Is the New Black*, *Stranger Things* and *The Unbreakable Kimmy Schmidt*. Perfect Moms are displaced by the eye-wateringly honest, jaw-achingly true to life, cringe-makingly real, *Workin' Moms*, and Alison Bell (who *always* chooses non-Good Girl roles) in *The Letdown*. *Jessica Jones* and *The Politician* present women as powerful and scary. In non-subscription TV, *Fleabag* schooled men in sex and love from the female perspective (THAT PRIEST) and *Killing Eve* (OK, just the first series) gripped us with the dissonant idea of a psychopathic woman; Kerry Washington and Reese Witherspoon initially vie for least likeable in *Little Fires Everywhere* (Reese wins hands down in the end); the very complex and very difficult Marianne in *Normal People* broke all the hearts of a captive Covid-19 audience. And we're even now seeing some very un-grey depictions of older women: Jane Fonda and Lily Tomlin in *Grace and Frankie*; Alfre Woodard in *Juanita*; Mary Kay Place in *Diane*; Judi Dench (now quite literally in *Vogue*).

In music, Billie Eilish, the anti-teen princess, expressed fury when a magazine made her look (to their minds) more attractive on its cover; Lady Gaga who was 'Born This Way' defies expectations with every new album (listen to *Joanne* now); Janelle Monáe made us re-appreciate the vagina in 'Pynk'; Queen Bey raises the game as leader of all female music superstars, continually rising higher and further above it all like the goddess that she is. Even Taylor Swift has morphed from the ultimate blonde and bubbly Good Girl to a self-aware and self-confident person in her doc *Miss Americana*. Watch it if only for the brilliant moment when she pulls herself up for apologizing when she 'soap boxes' about misogyny, with what feels like a Russian doll set of realizations: 'Was I too loud? In my own house? That I bought with my own money? That I made with the songs I wrote myself? About my own life?' New Taylor revealed in this documentary is a far cry from the seventeen-year-old who stood blinking back tears when Kanye stole her moment at the Grammys. Old Taylor stuck to the rules made for her by men in the music business; this one writes her own.

In film, you can follow the twists and turns of the listless Lady Bird, the furious Mildred Hayes in *Three Billboards*, the laugh-out-loud funny girls in *Booksmart* (Thirteen, you've come a long way from sitting around and taking House's abuse). You can see Amy reborn in Greta Gerwig's *Little Women*. In fiction, just read *My Brilliant Friend* – that will tell you all you need to know about just how difficult a clever woman, who's held back from realizing her potential, can be. And in non-fiction, the shelves are groaning with best-selling works of angry words (but often softly spoken like Michelle O's *Becoming*) such as *Invisible Women* (Caroline Criado Perez), *I Am Not Your Baby Mother* (Candice Brathwaite), *Bossypants* (Tina Fey), *My Life on the Road* (Gloria Steinem), *Yes Please* (Amy Poehler), *Difficult Women* (Helen Lewis) and *The Fix* (Michelle P. King).

Principle 3: Put an end to macho-economics

And – very handily when it comes to a suave authorial transition to the next principle – one of the places where exceptions are becoming norms is in economics. Here challenging female voices are creating hugely interesting and radical and insightful new perspectives that are shaking up male-authored doctrines and economic theory.

We've described how markets have developed over the time that we've been working: how we've gone from a growth era obsessed with globalization, macho bigger-is-best outlooks and a consumer climate that said more is more. How we then moved to a post-2008 era where – while there was quite a bit of wringing of hands about the dangers of unfettered capitalism and some denting of the faith in it as 'good for all' – things pretty much went on as they were but slightly offset by nods towards sustainability, conscious consumers and CSR-type 'initiatives'. But now we're moving to an era where new answers are required and where the contribution women are making to economic discourse will become increasingly influential.

An economics degree unlocks a lot of opportunities for the student: economics graduates earn £20k a year more than an arts graduate; in the US, economics majors are more likely than those in any other subject to head an S&P 500 company. Economists influence all kinds of policy-making that impacts the day-to-day health and financial wellbeing of the population. Practitioners contribute to social policy issues like childcare provision, income inequalities and education services. They are a powerful bunch. Less than one-third of economics students in the UK and the US are women (lowest in the world, by the way), and fewer again pursue a Masters in economics or a career in the field. Which must explain, at least in part, why the traditional economic model finds it so very hard to accommodate female priorities. And why so often it is women who bear the brunt of the growth objective with their predominance in low-paid jobs, and women who shoulder the impacts of the deprioritization of policy areas that don't impact men to the same degree (yes economist, it's childcare, stupid).

More recently however, we're hearing female voices emerge to challenge the traditional economic model. Women are proposing a new kind of economic model that is not enamoured (or at least not always enamoured) with growth, and which factors in social and environmental concerns. In particular, women want a model that doesn't necessitate the use and abuse of low-paid female workers. Those who are miles – metaphorically and literally – from the workers at the bottom of their supply chain might believe women in the UK or the US don't really care much about a woman they've never met in India. But women do empathize, because pretty much every single woman in the world knows what it feels like to be exploited or messed around by 'The Man'.

Kate Raworth develops these concepts in her much-praised book *Doughnut Economics*. In her thesis, Raworth visualizes an economic system using a doughnut. In the hole are the conditions necessary for humans to live good lives (food, water, education, dignity, access to healthcare). Capitalism, she suggests, should be deployed to deliver against these conditions for the whole population. Then in the doughnut ring is the 'sweet spot' (pun intended, presumably), where capitalism can operate and consumption can grow, but never beyond the point at which the scale of consumption hurts workers or damages the planet. Her thesis is growth-agnostic. Growth can be good, but it can also be harmful. You need to flex according to what the world needs, not according to last quarter's result.

In a similar vein, the Ellen MacArthur Foundation is championing the 'circular economy' and the 'cradle-to-cradle' design concept which means products from their inception minimize negative impacts on the environment and support consumer and worker health and wellbeing.

Mary Portas, who is a brilliantly insightful retailer, proposes the 'Kindness Economy' as a rather poetic solution to a system that fails to do the right thing by all:

> What we've come to realize as a society is that the tenets of capitalism, that 'more equals better', is not going to be better for us as people or for our planet . . . This new era, the Kindness Economy, is going to be about sentience. It's going to be about care, respect and understanding the implications of what we are doing.[35]

This new female influence on how the economic model gets mapped will deliver for women a more satisfactory response than the 'offsetting' approach which was adopted to avoid disrupting business as usual: airlines offset their fuel consumption; billionaires offset tax avoidance with philanthropy; supermarkets who present a threat to smaller shops offset with pretty paltry contributions to community charity projects; clothing retailers offset with a 'modern slavery' proviso at the bottom of their websites.

The female vision of the economy embeds social concerns into what was a circle that excluded them. The feminine version of the circular economy attempts to resolve what have often been set up in the traditional model as competing forces: workers' needs (dignity, fair pay, security and health) and consumers' needs (fair prices, quality products, good service, innovation). It tries to resolve financial objectives (growth to satisfy shareholders and employees, profit generation to deliver adequate pay levels and to reinvest) and social impacts (accommodation of workers' lifestyle needs; environmental impacts; community impacts).

This new economic model chimes with the way women are revising their purchase priorities (although admittedly they are not yet always acting upon them). We have been through a period of accelerated consumption, particularly in female-dominated categories, and by 2020 women were beginning to report that these higher levels of consumption felt far too frenzied to be healthy. Of course, Covid-19 soon put the brakes on that, as women were forced to reacclimatize to *not* buying – a new experience especially for younger women who hadn't gone through the deep recessions of the late twentieth and early twenty-first centuries. And when this habit of *not* shopping is added to women's already present anxieties about overconsuming, then 'buy less but buy better' is primed to become the new female consumer mantra. Brands will come to reflect the bigger economic vision that female economists have imagined: one where doing good and being a desirable product are no longer uneasy bedfellows.

We were already seeing brands occupy the premium end of the fashion market that roll into their business models the social impacts of what they do, so it will be interesting to see how this model extends out into mid- and low-priced sectors.

The Girlfriend Collective – which sells what it calls 'guilt-free fashion' – makes premium-priced sportswear (compression leggings cost £68) out of recycled water bottles. Not only is their performance-wear sustainable, they also guarantee fair wages, safe and healthy conditions and zero forced or child labour (we can only hope that such a promise will feel unexceptional before too long). They readily offer up their certification against these workers' rights guarantees on their website.

The Reformation, originally set up as an online-only eco-friendly brand in the US, is now a mainstream one. Everything is made in limited editions because all products are made using deadstock fabrics or repurposed vintage clothing, so the designers can produce unique ranges of clothes that satisfy the newly resourceful female customer who's expecting more than an off-the-peg that she'll see everywhere she goes (yes, we all remember 'that dress' with the spots from Summer 2019). Reformation has a substantial part of its website dedicated to the factories that make its product, in the US and internationally. A highly transparent approach is taken where factories that have violated any of the safety, health or labour regulations are called out on the website and are regularly audited and then excluded if improvements are not made. Originally expected to be a small and peripheral player, serving relatively few eco-conscious customers, Reformation now has three physical stores and has expanded its product range and team year on year. It is projected to triple its year-on-year sales in 2020.

We are already seeing treatment of women by businesses becoming not just an issue for fashion and beauty, where it is currently most prevalent, but for all packaged goods and services. We're already seeing Google workers make a global stand on the treatment of women by the company; we've seen Tesco workers file a case against their employer for paying women on tills less than men in the warehouse; cleaners and dinner ladies in Birmingham City Council have won the right to be paid the same as male street cleaners. And as brands continue to be evaluated against what good they do in the world, or at least how they manage the bad that they can, even inadvertently, cause in the world, we predict that a company's treatment of its female workers will soon become a new criterion for purchase (or a reason to boycott). Just as, ten years ago, businesses were compelled to demonstrate publicly their green credentials (remember Marks and Spencer's 'Because There's No Plan B'?), we foresee a moment, in the very near future, where the way in which firms treat their female employees will be scrutinized. We forecast the equivalent of a Trip Advisor that will tell women customers how companies treat their female employees emerging soon, akin to the Transparency Index from Fashion Revolution. And we predict women will exert their power as consumers and walk away from those companies who treat women badly – either as consumers or as employees.

Principle 4: Catch up with the expert

Recently we were asked to conduct a research project for a home-ware brand wanting to understand the changing ways in which women were consuming their category. The serried ranks of pressed-into-attending execs turned up, expecting that they could go through their emails in the usual way while listening vaguely to the discussion, occasionally muttering 'they often say that' whenever a respondent mentioned something that might be hard to implement. But, by the end of this discussion, those in our audience were not just listening, they were sitting up and thinking, simultaneously both stimulated and threatened by what they had seen and heard.

Because, during the discussions, women had described how they now bought the category, and the tools that they were using to make it work to their advantage. They described how they often spent two or three evenings a week roaming the internet, looking for ideas and inspiration. They explained how they used searches – particularly visual searches – to determine what they wanted and then where best to find it. They talked about their favourite influencers and the impact those influencers had on what they liked, and where they went to source it. They described how Instagram and Pinterest were the go-to places to see what could be done and how it could be achieved. They discussed where they went for hacks on how to achieve the ends they wanted, and they talked about ways of upcycling, changing it up and creating-your-own that they'd seen that allowed them to make those things for themselves. They explained how they shared voucher codes and brilliant deals with their friendship group. And, perhaps most powerfully of all, how they were happy and confident in going direct to source to get what they wanted. One woman described how she 'just went on a mission . . . I look and look until I see exactly what I want and then I know the price that I am willing to pay, and I'll just go online until I find it. I buy from little places, from wherever. You can always get what you want in the end.'

Another said, 'If you're willing to invest the time you can find it, you can always find it. You just keep looking, you can go everywhere online, just comb the earth basically until you get what it is you want.'

Another described how she had spent days researching and understanding the world of rugs before visiting a shop that she knew had what she wanted: 'I knew way more than the sales person in there. I knew exactly what I was after, how it was made, what the colours could be, everything. I thought to myself, don't give me that, I'm more expert than you are. I could work in this shop and wipe the floor with you with what I know.'

All of them described, how, one way or another, and by hook or by crook, they were using all the tools of the internet to get their own way: no longer on receive, they were tooling themselves up, arming themselves with the knowledge they needed to see through the patter, making their own solutions and sharing and supporting each other in achieving their own ends. They had become the expert – the very opposite, in other words, of the pliant, eager, impressionable student customer upon which brandsplaining approaches depend for their success.

While the seeds of this new resourcefulness were probably sown a decade ago, it is really only in the last few years that we have seen them blossom into a whole new era of resourceful female consumerism. The flowering of this new era has been facilitated and accelerated by the web, and in particular by the search and research tools that it has provided for women. In a new and hitherto unprecedented way, women can now work the system for themselves: seeking out what they want, sourcing how and where to find it and sussing out how to pay what they want to pay when they do.

This new era of dedicated inquiry and expert understanding

extends, of course, to a preparedness and an ability to look behind the scenes at what a company is really doing – and if and how that matches with what they are saying they do. Women are no longer prepared just to accept the front-of-house presentation; they're willing and able to dig deep to see if the talk is walked, and if what is being said is actually what is being done. And, again, the tools of the internet and social media mean that they are able to do this in a way that properly shines the light on the bullshit claims and misdeeds of both brands and, increasingly, influencers.

All of which tells us that time's up on the whole notion of a brand knowing more than its female audience, and talking down to them from a place of higher authority; the resourceful female consumer, tooled up by the internet and social media, no longer has to put up and shut up and pay up. The words spoken by that respondent about the rug shop service – 'don't give me that' – are now true in every sense. The newly tooled-up expert and resourceful female consumer no longer has to put up with what she's being given – whether that's shoddy service, condescending communications or bullshit pseudo-science.

Principle 5: Mend it for everyone

This next principle is about nurturing the sort of environment within business that allows understanding of women not just to be heard but to flourish: how we move on from the 'nothing to trouble your pretty head about here' masculine cultures that created the base settings, through the 'fix the women' era of the early twenty-first century, to something that is genuinely transformative. In her brilliant book *The Fix*, Michelle P. King sums up both the problem and the path to progress succinctly in the opening pages:

> the years we have wasted fixing women in the name of gender equality is simply time spent ignoring the inherent design flaws in most corporations. Instead, we need to look at the blueprints of our workplaces, to understand how the policies, processes, structures, employee behaviours, leaders and culture all enable a very small number of people to succeed.[36]

If businesses were more willing to listen closely rather than just 'glance' at the issue of gender inequality, they would hear that the problems sit with the organization, rather than with women. They would hear what we hear when we ask women about their slowness to progress in companies:

> Senior jobs involve doing things that are unnecessary to the successful fulfilment of that role, such as playing golf or going out drinking, and I don't want to do those things.
> The company has expectations based on the idea that most employees have stay-at-home wives taking care of the domestic

side of life, and I don't have a wife, I have a husband, who also works.

Because most companies think women do the domestic work, I'm overwhelmed because my partner has no permission from his work to help out at home, so I can't go for a promotion.

There are people in the company who believe leaders look and act in a particular way, and that particular way does not match with the way many women look and act, so I feel excluded, my confidence has been knocked as I've moved up through the company because I look and feel less and less like the people around me, so I'm thinking about leaving.

At the extremes, what would be revealed would be what the *Harvard Business Review* describes as a 'masculinity contest culture' which results in the kinds of alarming exposes we've seen in the last few years at Uber, Nike and CBS.[37]

Businesses have spent far too long trying to loosen the Gordian knot of gender inequality with things like workshops that help women overcome their (in fact quite valid) insecurities. Good leaders should instead slice right through that knot by addressing the failure of their company cultures and organizational structures to create accommodating environments for all, not just a very few.

When King talks about how the cultures and structures of organizations only enable a very small number of people to succeed, she suggests another truth that has been largely ignored until very recently, which is that it is not only women who find what she calls 'negative gender norms' in corporate cultures isolating.

Men are only pretending to be macho

That prototypically masculine cultures are alien to men too was described to us vividly by three men we heard speak at a conference recently. We thought the conference would be interesting because it was about 'bringing men into the conversation' about gender inequality. There were the usual presentations highlighting gender disparities (you know the sort of thing, full of depressing graphs showing small piles of pink figurative women and big piles of blue figurative men), and the conference followed the predictable pattern of PowerPoint slides to inspire and breakout groups to assimilate and discuss. It was very professional, but largely unsurprising, until three men took the stage. Each sat on a high stool at the front of the room, no slides, no cards. And each told a very individual story about their own struggles with the 'macho' culture of organizations they had worked in over their careers. Their stories were disclosing and their vulnerabilities laid out bare to the audience. They discussed difficult divorces, serious mental illness, their horror and sense of powerlessness when female colleagues were sexually harassed in work. None of them explained anything to the audience (of mainly women), they just shared their disenchantments with corporate culture and its inability to accommodate personal, human struggles. All three were working within their organizations to tackle what they could see were harmful beliefs about what kind of behaviour is acceptable at work and what is not. The final plea from one was, 'Look, we're the arseholes. We're the ones who are the problem. We made things this way and some of us are just working out that it's not great for anyone. You have to help change it because we don't know how to.' It was the revelations of that last session from these three men that felt like an approximate answer to the ways businesses needed to change if it's going to be possible to eradicate brandsplaining altogether as the marketing MO. Because, of course, the habit of explaining things to customers from a top-down perspective in marketing is born out of the kinds of cultures these men were describing.

Those cultures celebrate signals of 'top-dog' status and these characteristics leak out into the marketing they produce: knowing more, rather than feeling the need to listen and learn; using aggression or passive aggression rather than persuading or empathizing; committing to individual success rather than collective success. If men are going to share in the struggle to change the ways in which companies work, and in particular how they work for women, then success is much more likely.

Let the home into the workplace, and the workplace into the home

The investment that businesses committed historically to formal workplaces, and the contribution those workplaces were presumed to make to corporate culture, were called into question by the Covid-19 pandemic. Barclays Bank has already begun to doubt the requirement for big offices, and have noted how easily employees slid into working remotely. Major airlines like British Airways are downsizing because, among other reasons, businesses will be far less likely to fly their employees halfway round the world to attend meetings now that meetings via Zoom and Teams have proved to be effective alternatives. This shift away from inflexible, formal workplaces sparked by this crisis, which should really have happened as soon as 4G arrived, will have dramatic consequences for company culture.

This shift will move corporate culture forward. It occurs to us, when we visit clients' offices in Canary Wharf, that the buildings are a metaphor for so many of the problems those same clients go on to discuss with us. The experience feels designed to make you feel smaller and less significant than the company. As you approach the building you look skywards to the top floor, which seems to be somewhere up in the clouds; you stare up as you step onto a dizzyingly high escalator that takes you up and out onto an often vast reception area, where you peer over a high desk to be greeted by one of a team of identically kitted-out female receptionists. Then there's the inevitable awkward moment where your badge doesn't work and the glass barrier remains firmly closed, reminding you that you're 'the outsider'.

These vast constructs, and the mini ones that mimic them, are very soon going to feel positively weird. Imagine how alien they will seem to people as they re-enter 'normal' work, having been cocooned in spare bedrooms and plonked at kitchen tables in spaces filled with the smell of washing and cooking and the noise of children around. People have seen their CEOs in a brand-new light against the backdrop of their messy home offices and interrupted by disobedient children who do not yet realize that Mum or Dad is 'the boss'. The harsh and impersonal nature of the old corporate culture, where the domestic gets left at the door, will be thrown into relief by the soft chaos of home that people will have become accustomed to. New workplace cultures will need to bring some of that warmth of home, and a focus on care and empathy, to soften the culture of competition and performance.

More practically and more fundamentally, perhaps, the fact that fathers have been at home and mucking in (or at least mucking in a bit more) and taking part, means that the old order of women taking on the burdens of both home and work is going to be under serious review. Men have been given the opportunity to connect with their families in a way that wasn't possible when they were leaving the house to work every day, and they have been given the opportunity to properly appreciate the grindingly repetitive nature of the task that is keeping a home from descending into chaos. Those dual realizations will add their voices to what has been largely a female call for a change in the monolithic and inflexible way in which many businesses still work.

So, annoying as it may be that it takes male 'sponsorship' to move things forward, the fact that men now see both the benefits of being at home more, and the hard task that keeping the home going actually is, businesses might finally hear what women have been saying for a very, very, very long time. Good businesses will take this opportunity to mend it for everyone: to look anew at the way they expect both men and women to work. Provided working remotely has delivered similar productivity levels to being physically at work, they will build more flexibility into working practices so everyone can save time and reduce the stress involved in doing right by his or her family while doing right by her or his job.

Principle 6: Prepare for the primacy of female-made brands

This sixth principle is about looking at the development of brands when freed from the settings and constraints of male authorship.

Since 2010 – despite the fact that only 3 per cent of venture capitalist funds go to female-owned businesses – there has been a huge increase in female-founded brands in all kinds of markets. And they are challenging traditional brands that are failing to fire the female imagination. Gone is the opportunity of the 'lock customers in, and lock competitors out' dynamic that used to make the cost of entry too high for smaller, newer players. Huge consumer packaged-goods companies and health-and-beauty businesses used to be able to hook up with the biggest retailers to dominate shelf and floor space. The web, however, offers entrepreneurs an equal shot with a plethora of more targeted retail channels or, in the case of direct-to-consumer brands, the potential to be their own retail channel. Women have proven adept at deploying resources such as PR and new, more affordable media channels in order to connect and communicate with their customers. They have sold themselves in the level(ish) playing fields of crowdfunding, and finding Indiegogo much more receptive than Sequoia or Tiger. It's a hard slog to break through with a direct-to-consumer model when your competitors are spending millions on broadcast channels, but women, it would appear, are prepared to do that hard work and get it done.

And they're getting it done by conceiving of and executing ideas through a female perspective on their markets, not the default male one. They represent a direct threat to traditional brands by biting chunks out of their business. But perhaps their real power to transform lies in the way that they throw into relief the out-of-kilter way in which the established brands present women and present to women.

No market is more ripe for transformation than beauty, which for years, despite its almost exclusive use by women, was led and shaped by men. For years, women of colour struggled to find matches for their skin tone from brands offered by the big conservative, male-run beauty houses. You'll remember the Good Girl ideal is light skinned, of course, and so the tones on offer reflected that preference. In 2017 the singer Rihanna partnered with LVMH's incubator Kendo Holdings and responded to this massive gap in the market by launching Fenty Beauty. It offered forty different shades of foundation, at a mainstream accessible price point, to match almost every skin tone on the planet. Since then, some of the big make-up houses have reacted to the threat – L'Oréal launched True Match to catch up and keep up with this pioneering female line. And an array of brands have arrived on the market, proliferating choice (thank you Iman; Lipmatic; Mented; the Lip Bar; Bahi and Juvia's Place), and establishing make-up for women of colour as the mainstream idea it should always have been.

Emily Weiss, another example, was originally a beauty blogger and fashion assistant at *Vogue*. Her blog focused on users sharing information and advice around the products that they love – the perfect petri dish for examining female needs and desires. Hearing what women were telling her through the blog inspired her to create a new and even more ambitious business idea – one that could compete with the beauty industry head-on. In 2014 she secured investment from a venture capitalist, Kirsten Green (only 9 per cent of venture capitalists are women and Weiss was turned down by eleven before she got Green's attention who, presumably because she was a woman, could more easily share her vision). With this seed money she launched Glossier, a challenger brand to traditional players in make-up and skincare. Her millennial-friendly marketing and focus on social media as a channel to engage the audience gave her instant stand-out from bigger brands who were still 'splaining to women on TV and in female magazines. The initial product line was small and simple, contrasting with the hard-to-navigate branded alternatives: Soothing Face Mist, Priming Moisturizer, Balm Dotcom Salve and Perfecting Skin Tint Foundation. The copy style on the site is conversational and on the level, compared with the authoritative complexity and pseudo-science on competitor sites. And most importantly, the tone is positive and light – both visually and verbally. There is none of the angst or implicit criticism evident in competitor offers. It took four years for Glossier to turn into a $400 million business – by listening and asking instead of telling.

And banking, perhaps the most alpha male of all markets, received its first punch in the nose from a female-run competitor when Starling Bank was launched under the indefatigable leadership of Anne Boden. Boden had had a hugely successful career in banking and insurance across a number of companies and a number of countries. After taking a year out after the financial crisis in 2008, she says she realized that all of the things she had thought were true about banking and finance were, in fact, completely wrong. It dawned on her that the ways in which she had been seeing things through the lens of the banking establishment were out of date and at odds with what customers needed. When she took up her next role, at Allied Irish Banks, which had been bailed out post the financial crisis, an idea began to form. She conducted her own research, listening to female customers talk about how the banks had failed them and overcharged them, even when they were at their most vulnerable. She decided to set up her own bank, something no one did – or hadn't for three hundred years; it was certainly something no woman had ever done. A woman in her fifties (the age at which most women are put out to pasture in banking) seemed even more unlikely to pull it off. She wanted to create a bank that used technology to make banking easy and simple, that was going to be fair, that wouldn't overcharge, that would fit with the way people needed banks to be. The idea was so far out that she couldn't raise funds initially. Eventually, after three days of interrogation by a potential investor in the Bahamas, she secured £48 million – the biggest ever seed round – to launch the bank.[38] Perhaps the most remarkable thing about Anne

Boden when you hear her talk is her curiosity and humility, which means she is always listening and learning. The language she uses about the bank is completely different from the way big banks describe themselves. She talks about it providing the tools to make it 'the first really useful bank' – a modest-sounding, but very profound mission. Compare this with the pomposity of some of the mission statements described in Part Two. She talks about not punishing customers for making mistakes, but making banking fair for them. So, she's fixing the banks to suit the customers, rather than the other way round – radical! She's aiming for industry-wide transformation and talks about actively wanting banks to copy what she's doing, rather than TMing all over the place to protect her early mover advantage.

Let's move now from the big and grand world of banks to the small and private world of underwear. Here is where female-founded brands are right at home. This is a product sector where (only) women can really understand the pinches and the physical impacts of an ill-fitting bra or a pair of pants that are easily eaten by bum cheeks. Lively, the direct-to-consumer underwear brand founded by a former Victoria's Secret exec, Michelle Cordeiro Grant, provides a dramatic contrast to the male gaze of her previous employer. The brand features models but it also sources the women it features from the community of ambassadors who provide feedback, support and promotion for the brand. The fit guide is inspired and genuinely useful – it's about the experience of wearing underwear rather than the mathematics of measurement. Or Lonely Label, whose co-founder Helene Morris describes her line as a collection 'for women who wear lingerie as a love letter to themselves'. The name plays with the idea that lingerie is all about snaring a mate. Like Lively, Lonely Label features women as they are – in their own words, as it were. In the Lonely Girls Project – an ongoing photographic journal produced by the brand showing users wearing Lonely underwear – they are shown breastfeeding, lounging with friends or just very, very happy in their own company.

Leaving aside the individual successes these brands have had, their collective impact on our perceptions of what 'normal' looks like for women is a million miles away from the Good Girl presentations that dominate the traditional players' marketing.

The female-authored phenomenon is also behind the rise of influencers who are now graduating to full-fledged power-brand status. The influencer marketing industry is almost entirely female driven: 89 per cent of #ad posts are generated by women and 68 per cent of Instagram posts (the primary influencer channel users are female). These – what now have become influencer brands – enjoy the kind of committed relationship with their followers that most product brands can only dream of. In beauty, skincare and homeware, influencers are particularly powerful, making and breaking the success of products and brands. Zoella, the earliest and most successful influencer for the millennial audience, currently has over 12 million followers. Zoella's book *Girl Online* sold 78,000 copies in its first week, outstripping J. K. Rowling to become the fastest-selling debut novel of all time. Her transparency and openness about life as a young woman, dogged with all the anxieties and concerns that that entails, means that she mirrors her audience exactly, which in turn means that she easily wins the trust and affection of her followers. And they, of course, listen to her advice, not just about how to manage a panic attack but also which cleanser/mascara/pore concealer to buy. Her 'sell' is so much more convincing than a manufacturer brand's sell because she builds the relationship first, with her highly attuned female perspective, and sells the product from within the warm and comforting glow of the closeness she creates with her audience.

We see much the same relationship between Mrs Hinch and her followers. Now at first glance, Mrs Hinch is the anti-feminist and the perfect little Good Girl: she's blonde, curvaceous and perfectly turned out; her subject matter is housewifery, which could not be a more 1950s concern for women; she styles herself 'Mrs' as though her identity is entirely dependent on her wifely and subsequent motherly status. And yet, what Mrs Hinch does is to provide for women, who are still the ones primarily responsible for household chores and duties, a helpful stream of advice and sisterly encouragement when no one else seems to even notice that the dishwasher has been emptied. When we listen to women who are working and running their homes (which is most women) discuss this bizarre social media phenomenon #mrshinchhome, they are conscious that she's playing out an anachronistic idea about woman as housewife, and they can see how absurd her enthusiasm for cleaning is. But what they appreciate is her expertise in a subject that they find burdensome and boring and they enjoy her cheerful, buoyant and engaging way of talking about it. They like that she encourages them to buy cheap alternatives (like Zoflora) to the high-priced mass-manufactured cleaning products that the big brands offer. They love how she draws up intuitive house-cleaning timetables that make homecare less time consuming and more instantly impactful on the way their homes feel. She's useful, giving them advice that their mothers may have done, were they not living hundreds, perhaps thousands of miles away. She is neither ideological nor judgemental in the way she communicates and operates; she's there to serve her followers, not prescribe to them.

Influencers have been able to position themselves between brands and customers because brands have failed so far to pull off the trick that influencers do. They project from a female perspective and this builds trust, affection, loyalty and a willingness to listen. Women like Huda Kattan – who, according to the *New York Times* is the most influential beauty blogger in the world – and Chiara Ferragni – HBS founder of the Blonde Salad and nominated by *Forbes* magazine as the most influential woman in fashion, demonstrate how a positive, uncritical and inclusive approach is superseding the heavy, critical and excluding approach the traditional brands preferred to adopt.

When we ask women how they managed before social media, one woman likened her previous dependence on traditional media to 'feeling incredibly thirsty all the time and only being offered a couple of drops of water a day'. The limited space in newspapers

only allowed for the odd page to indulge women's aesthetic appe-
tites, especially as the editor had to squeeze in thirty pages of
coverage of men's sports. Specialist home magazines thick with
glossy pages were prohibitively expensive, and could also sometimes be less inspirational and more soul-destroying, as the editors
assumed a lifestyle and budget that most women barely recognized. The snooty 'designer lingo' language in the magazines also
turned women off. Their own homes had scuffed skirting boards,
yoghurt-splashed upholstery, unidentifiable stains on the carpets.
Women don't only want imagery that sets out wild aspirations
(although naturally they do want to see Mariah Carey's football-
pitch-sized bathtub), they also want attainable results, and most
interiors magazines or TV programmes couldn't offer that
combination.

Influencers, YouTube vloggers and internet bloggers, with their
breathy enthusiasm and helpful 'hacks', fit much more neatly with
what women want and need for their very real homes. Social media,
with its infinite capacities and multimedia platforms, features endless opportunities to browse and explore. If traditional channels felt
stingy with their offerings for thirsty women – in terms of both
quantity and quality – social media has served them a great big
glass of water.

Principle 7: Stop looking – and start learning

So, this seventh principle is about how to wire all that thinking and understanding into the organization – given that all businesses can't and won't be female made or even female led. We have discussed the dominance of male leadership in the marketing development process. While the number of female marketing directors has reached 33 per cent in the US and 45 per cent in the UK, we discussed how those marketing directors are often squeezed between two crucial roles in the development process that are overwhelmingly occupied by men: creative directors and CEOs. A prevalent 'masculine' culture operating in most big organizations acts as a kind of handbrake on progress in marketing, and keeps the brandsplaining MO in place. It's hard for female voices to be heard. It's hard for women to be *really* seen by businesses. We now need to get 'beyond the glance' to an approach that is properly deep-rooted, to find ways to really hear and see women.

Over recent years we've seen businesses in general – and 'insight' directors in particular – become preoccupied with Big Data. This love affair between marketing and terabytes kicked in properly when businesses developed the capacity to store masses of information (but not necessarily do anything with it) in the early 2000s. Tesco's ClubCard became the aspiration for every marketer in the world. Big Data would allow marketing to know everything about every single one of its customers with a granularity hitherto believed impossible. It could finally reduce customers down to the currency business likes to deal in – numbers. At the same time, there was a noticeable drift to more remote qualitative methods for understanding customer behaviour. Face-to-face qualitative research moved to online groups because they were cheaper. Viewing facilities became opportunities for sugar rush – both digital and real – rather than listening. Conversations with customers were replaced with more one-way, 'social listening', because it was super fashionable. And increasingly researchers were asked to make findings about consumers more digestible for the 'too busy to stop and take stock' marketing team. Short films summarizing customer groups started to replace longhand documents and presentations.

Of course, each method is perfectly valid when set against the right objectives (where would we all be without online research groups now?), but most of them don't give women the opportunity to put any misunderstandings or misinterpretations right – there is no inbuilt right to reply. And none of them deliver a deep, intuitive understanding of who the audience is (we will see what online groups can deliver when pushed to their limits over lockdown). Bearing in mind the prevailing male glance in play, this 'distance learning' of women is likely to have put additional fuel in the brandsplaining tank, just when a new approach was needed.

In this current context, the one where resourceful women are cantering off miles ahead in the distance with brands lumbering along behind, real insight is going to be required to catch up and keep up. And with the world on pause, there could not be a better time for businesses to review what they really know about women. If the pre-Covid-19 workplace culture operated out of a spirit of dominance, assuredness and strength, the new culture is operating out of a spirit of humility. Living with uncertainty and *not* knowing is becoming a new and crucial skill we are all having to learn. The world has been humbled by something microscopically tiny, and this will change our perspective on just how unassailable all our assumptions about the world really are.

One of the exercises we give women to do when we're trying to get under the skin of them is the Proust Questionnaire. You might not know it, but if it rings a bell, it is because *Vanity Fair* publishes a version at the back of its monthly paper edition. The premise (Proust's premise), is that if someone answers all the questions on the questionnaire, then the interviewer will know everything that there is to know about the interviewee. We're not sure that's absolutely true, but we do know that, given a safe space, it brings stuff up from right deep down in the female psyche – and yes there are tears here too. As an experiment, see if you could answer the questions confidently on behalf of your consumer audience . . .

What is your idea of perfect happiness?
Which living person do you most admire?
What do you consider the most overrated virtue?
What is your greatest extravagance?
What is your current state of mind?
If you could change one thing about yourself what would it be?
What do you consider your greatest achievement?
If you were to die and come back as a person, who do you
    think it would be?
What do you regard as the lowest depth of misery?
What do you most value in your friends?
Who is your favourite hero of fiction?
Who are your heroes in real life?
What are your favourite names?
What is it that you most dislike?
What is your greatest regret?
How would you like to die?
What is your greatest fear?
What is your most marked characteristic?
Where would you like to live?

In order to replace the 'male glance' on women with a deep understanding of them, we would suggest to any business owner an 'amnesty' period during which all the received wisdoms rattling around your business about what women think, and what they respond to, get put in a box somewhere for a while. Spend the 'amnesty' period studying women like you would a new subject. You can use Big Data, but make sure to involve little qual; you can do it online or offline – but however you have to do it, be at pains to create a context where you invite women's dissent, not just the surface responses, which often feel easy and agreeable. Start your exploration with a new-found sensitivity to the gender biases you may inadvertently be bringing. Don't get your team to synthesize the new understanding that emerges into a five-minute film or a few PowerPoint slides, so it fits neatly in your diary. Because you will want to get the helpful insight that lies between the lines and in the subtler shifts that are happening in female life and women's purchase behaviour. Understanding the contextual, the psychological and the emotional terrains of the female mindset will dramatically improve your ability to connect with women and deliver against their needs, and that is going to take some time.

Principle 8: Forget ideals – present a grounded and granular understanding

Brands – as we've described – first began at a place where they saw the female audience through a male lens and, as a result, centred on and presented back male-pleasing ideals. Over recent years, we've seen those ideals layered over with some 'token appearances' that glanced at other depictions of women and the lives they led. Now brands need to get beneath the surface and properly present women's lives as independent of male idealization, where women have the agency to make the calls and are no longer relegated to passive, dependent roles in which they are waiting to be noticed by men. And – following our principle of female voices and woman-made projects – there are lots of great (if still nascent) brands that provide illustration of what this could look like.

All the single ladies

A brilliant example of a brand that really understands the not-here-to-please-men audience is the jewellery brand Mejuri. The jewellery category – along with most others in the luxury space – has always been predicated on the idea of men giving to women. At a deep cultural level, the giving of jewellery by men to women has indicated possession and ownership: the man shows his power and wealth in his capacity to spend money on something both prized and non-functional; he bestows that power and wealth on a grateful woman who lacks the resources or agency to possess the thing herself. The engagement ring shows she has been chosen; the wedding ring shows she belongs to him; the necklace and earrings are adornments to decorate and enhance her appearance. Mejuri have seen and understood this age-old but now outmoded idea – and exploded it: 'Buy yourself the damned diamonds', the brand declares.

Noura Sakkijha – Mejuri's co-founder and CEO – understood that modern women weren't interested in waiting for a partner to think of gifting them something. Sakkijha came from an established Jordanian family business that had been making traditional jewellery for three generations, but the founding idea of the business came out of upending those established traditions. In an interview with *Glamour* magazine she describes how, 'when we founded Mejuri, our goal was to change the narrative surrounding gifting and to place the purchasing power into the hand of women . . . Now 75 per cent of purchases (at Mejuri) are made by women for themselves and for each other.'[39] The brand has a freedom and fun to it that is miles away from the stiffness and formality of the traditional jewellery brands: the tone is of liberation and enjoyment – made by women, bought by women for themselves and for each other. The patronage of men no longer plays a part in the equation: the positioning of the whole brand is predicated on the idea that women are no longer waiting for a man to put a ring on it.

Another female-founder brand born out of an understanding of the realities of modern female independence is the dating site Bumble. The brand was founded by Whitney Wolfe, who had originally been part of the team that set up Tinder. However, after a much-reported sexual harassment and discrimination lawsuit against Tinder (cue: a tirade of misogynist abuse against Wolfe in the Twittersphere), she set up Bumble, 'the first dating app where women call all the shots'. The idea of Bumble is that women have all the control: as with Tinder, users swipe right on a person's picture if they are interested and left if they are not, with two right swipes making a match. But there is then a crucial difference: once a connection has been made, only the woman can initiate conversation. She has twenty-four hours to send the man a message; if she doesn't, the match disappears. The only control the man has is the ability to extend one match each day for an extra twenty-four hours in the hope that the woman will respond to him given more time. It is almost a complete reversal of the age-old relationship mechanic where the woman waits, without agency, to be picked, and asked, and chosen.

In an interview with the *Telegraph*, Wolfe described the foundational thinking:

> I'm a strong, independent girl. But when it came to dating that was the one facet of life where I felt I wasn't allowed to go after what I wanted. I can do whatever job I choose, eat what I want, go to the gym when I want, but if I was out with my friends at a bar and saw a cute guy I couldn't go over and say hi. Women shouldn't be sitting back and waiting. It's so old-fashioned. I, for one, don't want to sit back and wait.[40]

On the website, the brand story is told with the same freed and freeing tone that informs many of the female-founded brands and reflects the outlook and spirit of their younger female audience:

> When I founded Bumble, it was because I saw a problem I wanted to help solve. It was 2014, but so many of the smart, wonderful women in my life were still waiting around for men to ask them out, to take their numbers, or to start up a conversation on a dating app. For all the advances women had been making in workplaces and corridors of power, the gender dynamics of dating and romance still seemed so outdated. I thought, what if I could flip that on its head? What if women made the first move, and sent the first message? Five years and countless Bumble weddings and babies later, we're a community of over 80 million across six continents. We've celebrated over 1.4 billion first moves. And we're just getting started.[41]

Looking back at historic ads for Diet Coke is an interesting way to illustrate the shifting attitudes of the audience – and the way that brands need to react to them. In its initial incarnation, Diet Coke came out of the binary light = female and full strength = male discourse. Coke was 'the real thing' shown in full-on red colour; Diet Coke was 'for the ladies' with the emphasis on weight control accompanied by a strongly flirtatious subtext that the aim of it all was to attract a gorgeous man. Later, the flirtatious Diet Coke drinker was presented as the watcher of men in the sexy construction worker ads (remember them?), where he's drinking and she's looking. As in much popular culture, the construct was based on a clunky first-base response to the problems of the male gaze: the simple reversal. Instead of men looking at hot women as sex objects, hot women would instead look at men as sex objects. Levi's played the same trick in its famous laundrette commercial. We saw it with Daniel Craig in *Casino Royale*, and Colin Firth coming out of that lake, and most recently Aidan Turner in *Poldark*. In the 2010s the Diet Coke brand moved on to a 'Girls, let's do this' sort of vibe – some slightly weird puppets called Eleanor, Bernadette and Irene were introduced and shown working in the fashion industry, mucking around in an all-girls-together, sub-*Sex-in-the-City* way, dancing on tables and generally talking about handbags. How very freeing. Then, after some wilderness years interspersed with lapses back to the leching-at-the-hunk approach (remember the one about the pool cleaner where the mother and the daughter and the boy next door all rush to offer him 'refreshment'?), the brand has arrived at a new 'because I can' place. In 2019 this was expressed by a Generation Z woman alone and talking direct to camera and insisting 'You can like what you like, because I can'. No man in sight. In 2020 it evolved to a 'You do you' campaign that aimed (apparently) to celebrate people being themselves, loving what they love and not caring about what other people think. The approach has (rightly, in our view) received a lot of criticism for its clunkiness (the line 'New year, same super-cute you' is particularly nauseating), but you get the idea of what they are trying to do: young women, freed from the shackles of male ideals, being just themselves. It may be crass but its intention is certainly an advance from its weight-shaming or male-objectifying forebears.

Unyummy mummyness

Popular culture derides the Perfect Mom now. Nobody wants to be Christina Applegate, the cookie-baking supermom in *Bad Moms*; they want to be Mila Kunis whose character is recently divorced and drinks a bit too much. Mothers are relieved to hear Chrissy Teigen open up about her post-natal depression and that she's happy to Instagram her squishy stomach and milk-filled breasts. *The Letdown*, *Motherland* and *Tully* present a lumpier, uglier, truer version of what the experience of motherhood is, and women say that feels really good. Ads that idealized mothers, with their billowing white sheets drying in the sunshine, were balanced out by Fiat's motherhood ad, in which a mother raps a 'warts and all' reality check on what motherhood really feels like.

A brand that has understood this new and more real presentation of motherhood is WaterWipes – a brand of baby wipe that the company describes as 'the purest baby wipe in the world'. There's lots of things that are notable and impressive about WaterWipes but one of the most refreshing is that it's a brand that's about parenthood, not just motherhood. Unlike the established brands, which, as we've discussed, continue to show mothers as the primary parent, Water-Wipes recognize that the preoccupying responsibilities (and the wonderful upsides) need to be shared. The brand's second notable characteristic is that it's about an honest depiction of parenthood. The website sets it out under the banner 'It's time to get honest about parenthood' and goes on, 'We believe it's time to be honest about parenthood. Because an honest conversation about the realities, is the first step towards self-belief. And with more than half of parents feeling like failures in the first year, something needs to change.' As well as the actual business of selling baby wipes, the brand has set up the #thisisparenthood project, designed to displace the idealized visions of parenthood, with all 'the negative impact that the dishonest representation of parenthood in culture and social media can have', with parents (as well as organizations, influencers and healthcare professionals) from all around the world sharing their real and unvarnished stories of parenthood, 'the ups, the downs, the laughs and everything in between'. The website features loads of little 'moment films' that explore the feelings that parents have about parenting. The films are headlined with sentiments like 'You hear people talk about this immediate love and affection and I did not feel that' and 'I still feel like a child myself', and it's a quietly radical project that, despite its slightly millennial hashtaggyness, is miles, miles closer to the reality of having a baby than the burnished, smiling, all-under-control Perfect Moms of the Good Girl era. Most radical of all, perhaps, is the fact that the brand was founded by a dad, which perhaps is the key to its refreshing perfection-free presentation.

The mommy blogosphere has also opened up space for a much more warts-and-all account of the realities of motherhood – and, increasingly, fatherhood. Although there is still a lot of pressurizing 'picture-perfect' content out there ('What do you get when you combine one NYC apartment, two parents, and five adorable children (including twins)? You get Love Taza, a quirky and adventurous blog created by Naomi Davis and her husband. Most of us can't imagine raising kids in the Big Apple, but Taza gives us an inside glimpse into their adventures as a family in the city. And as if city living wasn't exciting enough, the family also travels around the world, proving that adventures don't have to end when you have kids'[42]), there are now many dissenting voices, particularly with the rise of microblogging on Instagram, bringing not just a dose of reality to the whole thing but – drum roll – some intelligence and humour too.

Scary Mommy is perhaps one of the most famous 'success stories' that has come out of a counter-version of perfect motherhood. Created by Jill Smokler in 2008 from her kitchen table (obvs) in the suburbs of Baltimore, and sold seven years later in 2015 to Some Spider Studios keen to acquire the website's 6 million plus followers – Scary Mommy was initially revolutionary for its 'Confessions' feature that allowed users to post messages anonymously about the very un-perfect nature of motherhood. Describing itself as 'a community for imperfect parents', the monumental success of what is now, effectively, a massive global media brand, is its recognition – in some ways, celebration – of imperfection, and the slightly punky, maverick, outspoken editorial tone that validates it. Smokler believes that the success of Scary Mommy is rooted in its authenticity: 'Had I set out to create a parenting business, it likely wouldn't have focused on my shortcomings and failures – the very things that set Scary Mommy apart from every other site. Because it began with my personal stories, the tone of the site was very focused and defined. In a word, it was me.'[43]

Ilana Wiles's wildly popular blog *Mommy Shorts* is another very interesting example of a media brand that's demolishing the Perfect Mom, this time using humour rather than 'authenticity' as the sledge-hammer. Wiles, having left a career in advertising after having children (obvs again), began to publish essays, infographics and little bits of short film on the hilarity of motherhood. She went on to publish the *Guide to Remarkably Average Parenting* that became a *New York Times* best-seller. The blurb tells us that Wiles 'is not a good mother. She's not a bad mother either. Like most of us, she's normal. If you want solid advice about raising kids, this book is not for you. If you want to wallow in your own misery about how having kids is AWFUL, this book is not for you. This book pays homage to the every-parent and suggests that they are the people having the best child-rearing experience of all.' The idea of the every-parent is a fascinating and quietly radical one: parent not mother; normal not idealized; real not perfect; all of us not a stereotype; supportive not judgemental.

No more fade to grey

Sadly, there are no case histories to serve up here as exemplars of how to target this audience in a way that they would admire or want to engage with. And while it's sad, it's not surprising – the very fact there are no examples is an example in itself. The audience is completely overlooked and more or less disappeared: ageism really is the new sexism.

If you own a business, we suggest you begin at the beginning here, with a needs state analysis in your category for this audience. Get out there and listen to the ways in which you ignore them, or diminish them. Take it on the chin, and then start all over again.

And while you're getting all that underway, you can do the slightly less take-it-on-the-chin thing and read back issues of *Vogue*. Over the last five years, *Vogue* has been leading a pretty good charge when it comes to making the older woman visible. It's all been done in that graceful, smooth, velvet-glove way with which *Vogue* approaches more or less everything, but their call is actually quite radical:

> In recent years, the industry's rush to populate its shows with the new faces that appeal to teens and 20-somethings has led to collections filled with TikTokkers, Instagram models, and Hollywood starlets born after the Clinton administration. While there's nothing wrong with seeing a buzzed-about influencer livestream from the front row, Fall 2020 has reinforced the importance of talents whose value can't be measured in online metrics. There is a degree of authenticity that comes with the endorsement of women who have been longtime fans of a designer's work. Brands can barter with agents and management teams to ensure the presence of a starlet or viral star, but odds are that 83-year-old acting legend Vanessa Redgrave is not showing up to see a runway show unless she enjoys the clothes.[44]

To practise what they preached they've interviewed Jane Fonda, Meryl Streep, Tina Turner, Marie Helvin and Judi Dench – as well as putting out 'a special edition' (sponsored by L'Oréal) called the 'Non-Issue Issue', built on the belief (shared apparently by L'Oréal) 'that age should no longer be an issue'.

Principle 9: Be constructive, not critical

The primary lever for fuelling consumption in the brandsplaining model was making women feel that they had to be better or different from the way that they naturally are. In the foundation years, this presented as the perfectionist propositions, the critical eye, the pinking and blueing, the 'visible signs of ageing' style of narratives that created anxiety and 'not good enough'. This was then followed, in the apparently more benign era of the last fifteen years, as the brand telling women how to be different but doing it in a sneakier way: the indirect criticism, the assumption of moral authority, the silky (well, it was for shampoo) 'maybe change your behaviour a bit?' approaches. And all the while keeping the base-setting Good-Girl stuff going, in barely modified form, beneath.

But that's all over now. It's not about 'change this' or 'be that'. The primary lever to transform marketing to women in this era is simply this: hearing that women are good as they are, and working from that basis instead. To sum it up in as few words as possible – to be constructive rather than critical.

Treat positive subjects positively

Most women do love thinking about homeware, beauty and fashion (beauty and fashion are described as key interests for 80 per cent of women[45]), and those who have families almost without exception love the people in them dearly. They are not 'trivial' or unimportant subjects but the source of huge amounts of interest and satisfaction. Women's love for these subjects doesn't have to come from the fraught and anxious place that marketing often suggests it does and engagement with them doesn't have to feel like a fruitless, frustrating hunt. If marketing is going to be true to the way women actually relate to these areas of interest, there is no need for critical and punishing narratives. Because these subjects do not make women anxious. They are enjoyable, hobbyist, fun and highly, highly creative. So, the narrative needs to move on, because it's not working for women, and they don't want to hear it any more.

We discussed the fashion world's oddly authoritarian, rather grand and prescriptive approach to its market. In this new world of the resourceful female consumer – consumers who are looking for creativity and constructive narratives – few women will ever seek to fill these prescriptions. You may never have heard of Lidewij Edelkoort, but she is the most renowned trend spotter in the fashion world and works with all kinds of businesses to help them forecast and therefore manage a murky and mercurial world. She predicts a near-view future where women no longer listen to brands that tell them what is 'in' and what is 'out' – even ones run by Karl and Tom. She writes in her manifesto – 'Anti Fashion, a Manifesto for the Next Decade':

> The consumers of today and tomorrow are going to choose for themselves, creating and designing their own wardrobes . . . they will rent clothes, lend clothes, transform clothes and find clothes on the street . . . they will build up their wardrobes and mix last year's basic with next year's must-haves and grandmother's Kelly with daddy's neckties to give it all a contemporary edge.[46]

The idea that women will be told by a group of very distant (in every possible sense of the word) men what perfect looks like is – at least to her mind – risible.

Beauty and fashion are ready for a radical rethink, and the thing its leaders have to do is reassess what they think they are in the business of doing for women. Appearance matters to women but the vast majority – 78 per cent[47] – would rather be praised for their minds than their looks. When asked what they believe defines them as people, intelligence is the highest scoring quality with appearance falling far, far behind it. Remember the top-scoring lifetime aspiration amongst women, in our study, was 'to feel comfortable in my own skin' (at 68 per cent). Marketing has to stop treating the subject like it's deadly serious, a matter for elation or depression, which feels critical and destructive. Left to their own devices and without the interference of the once male-run beauty industry, women would treat it as a constructive, light and fun subject.

Women say they find beauty and fashion engaging because they find these interests inherently creative and use them as a method to express themselves. A fleeting glance at Instagram will reveal Gen-Z girl teens 'trying on' different identities, tooled up with the kind of professional-level make-up know-how and expertise their grandmothers could only have dreamed of. One minute they are a VSCO girl (oversized sweatshirt, cat line, scrunchie on her wrist beside a Pura Vida bracelet, a penny board and the VSCO classic – a Kanken backpack), the next they're a Soft Girl (anime inspired, Bambi eyes, pastel blush, glitter, pink wig), then they transform into an E girl (mesh T-shirts, colourful hair clips, Sailor Moon skirts and O-ring collars). In some TikTok videos they are all three, morphing from one to the other. Women mess with K-Beauty (luminosity), follow eyebrow styles (bye, bye Cara) and pre-order Kylie's lip glosses, because it is a distracting *process*; it's the 'making of' that's enjoyable for women, not really the end result (which is more often than not so far from the promise). Play value and creativity are the driving forces in make-up and skincare and brands that get this set out to amuse and entertain women rather than undermine them.

Female entrepreneurs seem to have an intuitive understanding of the need for a more creative constructive approach to beauty and fashion. Check out Beauty Bakerie for a taste of its positivity. It was launched in 2011 by Cashmere Nicole and is a story of pure female resilience. Nicole, a single mother who put herself through college and nursing school, found she still hankered after a working life that revolved around her interest in art and business. When she conceived of the brand, which is about as pink, frothy and fun as a brand can get, she set raising awareness of breast cancer as a primary objective for the business. Within a year of setting it up, she herself was diagnosed with breast cancer, but continued to build the business despite having to undergo a double mastectomy. She developed products that are vegan, non-toxic and cruelty free in part because as a cancer survivor she was highly attuned to concerns around toxicity. She made efforts to crowdfund the business, which were given a huge female-fuelled boost when Beyoncé featured the brand and told Nicole's story on her own website. Visiting the site is a 100 per cent feelgood experience. The delicious-sounding names of the products don't nod to flaws in the user but tempt her with the promise of sensory pleasure (Crème Lip Whips, Cake Pop Lippies, Eyelash Icing, Proof Is in the Pudding Eyeshadow palette). The central 'smudge proof' promise in her products is telling too. It points to a flaw in other make-up lines, which can slide straight off the face at the first appearance of a bead of sweat. Nicole doesn't assume women are sitting still while looking beautiful, but rather they are sweating while they're running for a bus, or rubbing their faces thoughtfully while busy working at their desks, so need something with more capacity for staying put. By 2015, because users found her positive narrative magnetic, Nicole had secured a $3 million investment from Unilever Ventures and the business now has a revenue of $5.4 million and is profitable.

In fact, the language deployed in almost all female-run direct-to-consumer beauty brands feels constructive and creative rather than critical. Pat McGrath Labs is like a one-woman art show, but featuring make-up. When you pop onto Juvia's Place the 'subscribe pop-up' announces to you that 'you are magic'. AYR – a fashion brand set up by three women in fashion in 2014 – couldn't care less for the trends set at the heart of the fashion industry. The name stands for All Year Round, 'seasonless essentials for everyday life'; legitimizing the idea of buying what provides comfort and confidence rather than buying what you are told you should be wearing.

When women tell you that something needs fixing, assume that they mean it and then do it

There's a joke that appears in almost every episode of *Modern Family*. Phil trips over a loose stair, looks guiltily to camera and says '[must] fix that step'. The reason it is good enough to feature so regularly is the truth in it. At any one time, every household will have one job that needs doing (by the 'man of the house'), but never, ever actually gets done. If brands don't respond to women when they tell them they don't like stuff about the category, or its marketing, or its service, they're being just like Phil. Only without the humour. 'Yeah, yeah, we'll get around to that' (never).

So, OK, it's time to get around to fixing your equivalent of the loose stair that women have been 'mentioning', probably for years.

Anne Boden's aims in setting up Starling Bank were to right the wrongs in the market for all consumers, but with a particular interest in how financial services treat women. A recent campaign from the bank was typically shape-shifting in the way it presents the problems with the way the market treats its customers: 'You're not bad with money, you're just with the wrong bank' was the empathetic statement on Starling Bank's billboards on the London Underground in 2019, and it launched a Twitter campaign with the very constructive hashtag #feelgoodaboutmoney. For years, women were told that the reason they didn't have any cash was that they just didn't know how to handle it. Starling, in contrast, admitted that it was the opacity and clumsiness of the tools financial services offered that made it difficult for anyone to feel in control of their finances.

Over the years that we have been working in the female consumer space, we've been constantly reminded, in almost every category that we've ever researched, that women strongly favour brands that actually do things. In particular, they admire brands with a practical heart: ones that genuinely set out to help, that create order, that make things easy, that help take the weight off. The mirroring of their own resourceful outlook is recognized and respected; in this context, actions genuinely do speak much louder than words.

Brands that genuinely wish to connect with women should not only talk about supporting them but also put their backs and their budgets into actually doing it. To date, we've seen the success of this sort of approach with some of the femvertising brands who – instead of just putting their missions on the wall and leaving them there as 'statements' (the clue is in the name) – have actually put them into practice. We see it with Dove's ongoing tradition of activism (again, action – the clue is in the name), most recently in their brilliant #ShowUs project where they've partnered with Getty Images and Girl Gaze to create a library of images of women and non-binary individuals that push at the boundaries and conventions of received wisdom around women. We see it in the work of the new female-founded brands that build their offer and their products out of a constant hands-on process of working with, and talking to, their customers. So, brands like ThirdLove, whose founders were frustrated by 'lousy bras and bad fits' and set out to create their lingerie based on actual measurements of actual women. As they describe it:

> We do bras differently. No discomfort. No dressing rooms. No drama. Just insanely comfortable bras, designed to fit perfectly. We use millions of real women's measurements – not size templates – to create our products. Our Fit Finder recommends your ideal bra in 60 seconds. In between cup sizes? We invented half cups. We carry double the amount of sizes of most other brands. We make it our mission to make a bra for you.[48]

And ThirdLove are massive activists too: when, in 2018, the chief marketing officer of Victoria's Secret gave a very brandsplainey interview to *Vogue* justifying the fashion show, Heidi Zak, co-CEO of ThirdLove wrote an open letter that was published in the *New York Times*:

Dear Victoria's Secret,

I was appalled when I saw the demeaning comments about women your Chief Marketing Officer, Ed Razek, made to Vogue last week. As hard as it is to believe, he said the following:

'We attempted to do a television special for plus-sizes [in 2000]. No one had any interest in it, still don't.'

'It's like, why doesn't your show do this? Shouldn't you have transsexuals in the show? No. No, I don't think we should. Well, why not? Because the show is a fantasy.'

I've read and re-read the interview at least twenty times, and each time I read it I'm even angrier. How in 2018 can the CMO of any public company—let alone one that claims to be for women—make such shocking, derogatory statements?

You market to men and sell a male fantasy to women.

But at ThirdLove, we think beyond, as you said, a '42-minute entertainment special.' Your show may be a 'fantasy' but we live in reality. Our reality is that women wear bras in real life as they go to work, breastfeed their children, play sports, care for ailing parents, and serve their country.

Haven't we moved beyond outdated ideas of femininity and gender roles? It's time to stop telling women what makes them sexy—let us decide. We're done with pretending certain sizes don't exist or aren't important enough to serve. And please stop insisting that inclusivity is a trend.

I founded ThirdLove five years ago because it was time to create a better option. ThirdLove is the antithesis of Victoria's Secret. We believe the future is building a brand for every woman, regardless of her shape, size, age, ethnicity, gender identity, or sexual orientation. This shouldn't be seen as ground-breaking, it should be the norm.

Let's listen to women. Let's respect their intelligence. Let's exceed their expectations. Let women define themselves.

As you said, Ed, 'We're nobody's ThirdLove, we're their first love.' We are flattered for the mention, but let me be clear: we may not have been a woman's first love but we will be her last.

To all women everywhere, we see you, and we hear you. Your reality is enough. To each, her own.

Heidi[49]

It is cutting through the crap, on the level and on the side of their customers, daring, outspoken, funny, and all about deeds not words (although, in this instance of course, the deeds were the words).

This practical, getting-on-with-the-job and making-yourself-useful approach is a hallmark of many of the other female-founded brands. Universal Standard is a good case in point. It was set up by Alex Waldman and Polina Veksler, two women with a very clear sense of the job that needed to be done: the average woman in both the US and in the UK wears a dress size 16, yet the options and the shopping experience for them was, in their words, 'dismal. It was clear all women weren't given the same level of style, quality or even respect'. So they set about addressing the problem – creating a clothing line of practical style basics that the *Independent* has called 'the most size inclusive clothing line ever'.[50] All their clothing is available in US sizes 00–44 (UK sizes 4–44) and the way they sell is replete with approaches that are genuinely about helping. Online there's a 'See it in your size' facility that enables customers to see items being worn by models of their own size (rather than just the usual skinny showy form), and there's a service called Fit Liberty that recognizes the everyday truth that women's weight fluctuates and, on that basis, promises that if your size shifts up or down within a year of purchase, they'll exchange the item for the new size for free. And then they donate any returned items to organizations that support women getting back into work and achieving economic independence. This immensely practical, problem-solving, action-orientated approach is so demonstrably different from the standard, take-what-we-tell-you ways of the fashion industry, and comes out of a desire to deliver for the customer; as one of the company's values states: 'at the heart of what we do, is you. Our goal is to consistently elevate and ultimately exceed your expectations . . . we don't just look out for your reach-outs, we look forward to them. No request is too small or favour too great. We're here to make you happy. Seriously. Try US.'[51]

And, in the period-products space, there's a whole host of female-founded brands – Knix, Thinx, Dear Kate, Ruby Love – that are setting about the practical task of making the messy business of periods easier. All of them have approached the market with a problem-solving attitude: how to make having a period more comfortable (both emotionally and physically). Knix was started by Joanna Griffiths after she first experienced the realities that women face post-childbirth. After talking to hundreds of women about what was wrong and where help was needed she concluded that female underwear generally 'had too much frill and not enough function' – and set about creating a line of leak-proof underwear that was both comfortable and pretty. Since then the brand has extended into all areas of underwear but always with a focus on practicality and comfort – they are now 'the world leader in wire-free bras and functional underwear'. Dear Kate sets out to do a similar thing: clearly recognizing that 'life still happens' and then setting out 'to find an alternative to simply putting up with life's leaks and stains'. Ruby Love is on the same sort of mission: why, asked the founder Crystal Etienne, should we 'settle for products that were designed decades ago, are uncomfortable and that fail us constantly? Why give young girls objects – that are often riddled with chemicals – to insert into their bodies? Why stress over the embarrassment and shame of leaks and stained clothes?' The answer to those questions was a range of period swimwear, nightwear and underwear all designed to solve the problem, and to solve it in a supportive, intelligent way. In this way, these brands actively mirror and reflect the attitude of their audience: just like the women they serve, these brands are, themselves, resourceful, knowledgeable and tooled-up.[52]

*Women are clever and funny, so the least you
can do is be clever and funny too*

At the risk of treating you, dear reader, as lacking in intelligence and agency, you'll remember how, in the earlier part of the book, we described the patronizing nature of the creative vehicles traditionally used to talk to women, and what they communicated subtextually: the infantilizing tones and colour palettes that say 'you're like a child'; the literal slice-of-life creative vehicles that say 'you can't deal with complexity'; the blithe hair-swinging characterizations that say 'you're gullible and unthinking'; the endless casting of beautiful women that say that 'how you appear is more important than what you do'; the supporting roles in the narrative that say 'you're secondary and there to serve'; the improbably grateful appreciation of the brand's performance that says 'we're the master in this relationship'.

And, in more recent times, the often condescending tropes of femvertising: the mournful, monochrome, charity-case vignettes (invariably accompanied by a plaintive piano soundtrack) that say 'you need to be helped'; the single triumphant woman showing her strength that says 'be more like a man'; the lazy repetition of the sub-*Sex-in-the-City* line-up of women of different shades and shapes that says (with a yawn) 'OK, we've ticked the boxes. Everyone happy now?'

And then, finally, the stuff that's barely ever shown: women being funny; women being clever; women being the protagonist in the narrative; women telling men; women being disobedient; women being angry; and we're on repeat now, the absence of older women.

As starting points for both progressive propositions and enlightened presentation, it is useful to look at how women see themselves – and how they want to be seen. Remember that, in our 2019 study, we saw that there were whole areas of female aspiration and presentation that were barely touched by brands or their agencies. Most striking was the finding that 76 per cent of women – and remember this is across the globe, across age groups, and across socio-demographic groups – agreed with the statement 'I'd rather be praised for my mind than my looks'. But looking at the composition, character and content of most female brands you would have absolutely no idea that this was the reality; in fact, you'd be much more likely to conclude the opposite – that women were overwhelmingly preoccupied with their appearance and paid scant attention to their intelligence.

Almost as surprising – given the pleasing, conformist Good Girl tones of the majority of female brands – was the finding that 78 per cent of women 'feel that it is now more acceptable for women to be outspoken and bold'. Again, you would never conclude that was the way women felt by looking at the brands that claim to be designed to speak to them. And there are other territories that remain almost entirely unexplored by female brands: over 60 per cent of women want to be seen as kind, 56 per cent as helpful, 41 per cent as funny.

To underscore just how lopsided and disrespectful the approaches are, it is helpful to contrast them with those employed when the audience is male. Here we see almost the mirror image of the relationship between brand and audience that we see with women: in the male discourse, the audience is typically 'the master' and the brand is almost invariably 'at his service'. In male categories, the audience is regularly considered or shown as 'in charge': the visionary, the adventurer, the joker, the sage, the warrior, the triumphant (in one way or another) hero. And the brand is there to facilitate and support his achievements: to get the girl, to take to the open road, to quench his thirst, to accompany and celebrate his sporting triumph.

And the creative techniques and vehicles that are used to present these heroic promises are, almost invariably, much more highly developed and sophisticated than those used when the audience is female. Think of the production values, the humour, the soundtracks and the special effects: the audience is respected enough for the authors to understand they need to be entertained and engaged. There's no assumption that the audience will be on receive – the willing student eager to be told. In fact, the opposite is true: the viewers are worldly, challenging, knowing and wise and need to have the creative red-carpet rolled out if there's to be any chance of engaging them.

Be straightforward

And precisely because they are worldly, challenging, knowing and wise, women can't be bullshitted. The sleight of hand in marketing of the past has created a following who know what's going on – so the brand must put aside grandiose purpose, big claims, bamboo-zling language and all the better and 'holier-than-thou' approaches that have informed the old ways, and instead just behave in a straightforward manner where everything is open, honest and on the level.

The Ordinary skincare brand is a great example of this on-the-level approach. In a category that, as we've described, has been predicated on insultingly preposterous claims and more-or-less made-up scientific language, the straightforwardness and the modesty of The Ordinary is conspicuous. The Ordinary's offer is completely stripped back – no unnecessary packaging, low-key pack design, no misleading ingredients bollocks, more or less – and in this case very much less – just the product. Interestingly, in the company's explanation of itself and its purpose, there's very little grandeur or magnificent shoot-for-the-stars ambition: it's all much more modest and much more down to earth. 'The Ordinary is an evolving collection of treatments offering familiar, effective clinical technologies positioned to raise pricing and communication integrity in skincare. The brand was created to celebrate integrity in its most humble and true form.' In fact, in complete contrast to the perfectionist promises and standard grand claims of the industry, the brand is completely open about the fact that there's nothing incredible or transformative about its product at all. What makes it special is its modesty and openness: 'Its offering is pioneering not in the familiar technologies that it uses but in its honesty and integrity. The Ordinary is born to disallow commodity to be disguised as ingenuity.'[53] In so doing, the brand treats the audience not as dumb saps to be fed 'the science bit' but as intelligent, thinking women who are knowing enough not to buy the bullshit.

Milk Makeup is another pretty good example of a modern female (and female-founded) brand that dispenses with the idea that the audience need things explained to them and instead treats them as funny, clever and knowing. Set up by four New York women, the offer is (to use the word much favoured by Gen Z-ers) completely 'clean' and, like The Ordinary, comes in packaging that is pared back and straightforward (if a bit less medical). Again, the brand focuses on the space it occupies – the place where beauty meets utility. One of the co-founders, Zanna Roberts Rassi, described in an interview how, as a brand, they always set out by thinking about what they are actually going to *give* to the customer, and to do that in a way that doesn't depend on bullshit. The principles behind the brand are, effectively, all about editing out excess of every kind: 'I know just how many millions of products there are out there, all promising something. I wanted to literally edit, with no excess . . . It's all about "the take-away".'[54] And again, the brand knows its place in the life of the audience: it's not about the 'big I am' purpose statements but about being useful, being clear, being straight, and being on the level. The copy on the website lays it out:

> Life is full of unknowns. Where are my keys? How did I stain my shirt already? Can I live off of dry shampoo alone? While we can't necessarily give you answers to those questions, what we can do is be upfront with you about what we put into, and leave out of, our products. Milk Makeup is all about good ingredients and epic payoff. That's why we want to be transparent with you. The below list will tell you about the ingredients that we promise never to use, the manufacturing and testing guidelines we adhere to, and the allergens and irritants that don't make the cut. We hope you find this a helpful resource, and, more importantly, we hope you get that stain out before your meeting.[55]

And then, of course, there's Rodan + Fields: those of you reading in the US will probably know all about it, but for those of you who aren't, it's actually the number one skincare brand in North America, with a company valuation, according to Euromonitor, of $1 billion. This too is a brand founded by women (two Stanford-trained doctors, Kathy Fields and Katie Rodan) for women, but what is interesting about it in on-the-level terms is that it's also actually sold by women; Rodan + Fields is not distributed via the classic retailer route to market but, in a digitally led update of the old Avon Lady formula, is sold through a peer-to-peer network of female 'consultants'.

For those of you who don't know the story, we'll quickly bring you up to speed. Kathy Fields and Katie Rodan are both practising dermatologists who were friends at college. In 1989, when they were both working at separate male-dominated practices in California, they got together to create an acne-treatment that they called Proactiv. After having zero success in their efforts to engage the big beauty or pharma companies in their offer, they finally 'settled' for the distinctly unfashionable 'infomercial' route to market. This channel – which represented the absolute opposite of the glamorous glossiness of standard distribution channels – proved to be astonishingly effective: Proactiv became their distributor's best seller and both the company and their rights were later sold to Nestlé, reportedly for upwards of $50 million.

Having created one best-selling brand and a nice fortune to go along with it, you could have expected the pair to shrug off their lab coats and take in the California sunshine. But they didn't. Driven by a purpose, they both opted to carry on with their work because they felt a genuine need to solve people's skincare problems. In an interview with *Forbes* they described how 'our motivation was solely for that need. We didn't dream of a business and an office.'[56] Perhaps as a result of that very hard-working and humble sort of approach, the new line that they created – Rodan + Fields – was another success and was bought by Estée Lauder a year after it was launched.

But interestingly, the brand did not flourish in the conventional hands of the Lauder beauty giant, and after five years the two founders decided to buy the brand back. Once it returned to them, the unpretentious and down-to-earth approaches they had originally pioneered also returned: they decided to sell Rodan + Fields products via the comparatively unfashionable and unglossy route of women selling to other women (or, to give it its distinctly grandiose proper title, via a multi-level-marketing structure). This route proved amazingly successful and, while there's a bit of sniffy push back around pyramid selling attached to the success story, the results, as they say, speak for themselves. While the brand is targeted at an older market sector, and at a higher price point, than The Ordinary and Milk Makeup, their success is based on the same common ground: they're on the level and down to earth, straightforwardly working to serve (rather than to master) their female customers in a way that respects their intelligence and credits their resourcefulness.

Treat gender as performance

For the younger female audience, gender has little to do with biological sex. Only 10 per cent of women aged sixteen to twenty-four across the world believe that gender is a characteristic that defines them. Over half of this audience believe that gender will be irrelevant in the future. A burgeoning gender vocabulary is freeing this generation from binary definitions and allowing for much greater self-expression and experimentation. Whether this youthful audience is cis, gender queer, intersex or one of the many other ways in which they could pin themselves on the gender landscape, increasingly they feel comfortable playing around with the concept. Regarding gender as performance, rather than something fixed and tied to a biological turn of events in the womb, opens up a whole new palette of possibilities for marketing.

Make Up For Ever was founded by professional painter and sculptor Dany Sanz, originally to offer professional quality products to make-up artists in the fashion and film industry. Completely free of the critical, perfectionist, male-pleasing narratives of traditional beauty brands, Make Up For Ever is centred on the belief that 'life is a stage' and make-up is an art form for expressing personality, character, individualism and mood. In describing its philosophy, the brand takes a stance that's the opposite of the boxed-in bell-curve ideals that are at the foundation of the traditional beauty brand: 'people are the artists of their own lives . . . The brand considers make up a means of self-expression and invites its tribe to play, experiment and ultimately re-discover their inner artist . . . the brand teaches everyone to free their personality and to discover and claim their true selves.'[57] The brand was acquired by LVMH and last year appeared in the *Forbes* list of the top twenty most influential beauty brands.

Also on that list is another brand, Morphe, that sets out to (slightly cringey line but its heart is in the right place) 'blend the rules'. Again, the positioning is all about stepping outside boxes and away from the restrictive boundaries inherent in binary thinking: 'At Morphe, there are no rules. Stereotypes? Not interested. We're real all the way. Dare to create. Push those boundaries. Make an impact. Show the world your true, vivid, exploding colours. You do you. And no one else.'[58] *Forbes* and *Vogue Paris* put Morphe third on the list of the most influential beauty brands, with a media impact value (a metric they've developed to quantify how a brand generates value) of $346,998,027.

In the same way, this sixteen-to-twenty-four age group also responds to brands that take a gender-neutral stance. Fashion has always been about self and group expression, and now we are seeing the emergence of brands that are no longer simply categorizing their clothes into two genders. Nicopanda is a New York-based streetwear brand that sets out its stall around the three values of diversity, inclusivity and creativity. The brand was founded by a man, Nicola Formichetti, who is something of a legend in the fashion space: he is highly acclaimed within the industry for his work in various top design roles at, amongst others, Uniqlo and Diesel, but is best known to non-fashionista mortals for his collaborations with Lady Gaga, including the magnificent barrier-busting meat dress. Having noticed a trend of girls and boys switching clothes, he set out to bring the idea of unisex clothing to a mainstream market. The brand's clothing is effortlessly ungendered – the clothes are just brilliant clothes, and who wears them and how genuinely feels as if it is neither here nor there.

Another clothing brand that's doing interesting genderless work – admittedly at the leading edge – is Agender, which, as the name suggests and the website tells us 'can be literally translated as non-sexual'. The site is organized along entirely neutral lines – with tabs for Tops, Bottoms, Outwear and Knitwear – and the clothing and models all resist gender definition. The same 'romantic checked shirt' is worn by a boy and a girl: the 'minimal track jacket' is, well, just a minimal track jacket.[59]

And it's not just new, leading-edge brands that are promoting this new way of thinking about fashion and clothes – the luxury brands are on it as well. Saint Laurent, Burberry, Tom Ford, Tommy Hilfiger and Haider have all combined menswear and womenswear runway shows, and Gucci shows now often have female models wearing clothes from the men's collections and vice versa. Gucci have, in fact, been particularly active in this space with a campaign for gender equality called 'Chime for Change', and a short film called *The Future is Fluid* presented at the Sundance Film Festival that is worth a watch on YouTube.[60] Gucci have also launched a gender-neutral fragrance called Mémoire d'Une Odeur (clearly the ridiculous pretension that defined that category hasn't been abandoned at the same time as losing the hyper-gendered imagery) that featured a gender fluid cast and, we are told, 'transcends gender by its individuality'. We may all feel a bit cynical that these approaches are no more than the usual Zeitgeist-chasing, attention-seeking behaviours of the notoriously intra-competitive fashion world, but, at the very least, they represent progress away from some of the incredibly limited, male-gaze approaches of the past (yes, Carolina Herrera, you may well be looking at your shoes at this point, hoping we won't mention your 'Good Girl Eau de Parfum' that is sitting, unashamed, right there on the counter of Boots).

And, as ever with fashion, the old rule of the leading edge trickling down to become next season's mainstream applies. Last year, we saw H&M launch a gender-neutral clothing collection with Swedish label Eytys. Entirely unisex, the collection had a traditional workwear feel to it and, again, function and utility were to the fore. One of the designers, Max Schiller, described it as 'a design philosophy of robust and fuss-free design where function triumphs embellishment and styles spans gender'.[61] And H&M aren't alone: Uniqlo, Zara, Urban Outfitters, they're all doing it, pointing the way to an emergent future that properly recognizes and reflects the fact that 38 per cent of Gen Z-ers 'strongly agree' that gender no longer defines a person, and only 14 per cent of young women believe they are totally feminine.

What's interesting about these shifts towards more unisex approaches in fashion is that the identities that are being projected in the clothes and their presentation are often more to do with action than appearance. Tracksuits, sweatshirts, T-shirts, trainers, lace-up shoes for walking, jumpers for warmth not just style, all point to a possible radical place where identity is less about how women look and more about what they do. That old foundational rule – expressed so brilliantly by John Berger: 'Men act and women appear. Men look at women. Women watch themselves being looked at. This determines not only most relations between men and women but also the relation of women to themselves. The surveyor of woman in herself is male: the surveyed is female. Thus, she turns herself into an object of vision: a sight'[62] – is being challenged, with consequences that feel more profound and longer lasting than simply the fashion industry being fashionable.

Principle 10: *Acknowledge that sexism goes both ways*

As we've discussed throughout this book, the discourse to date has largely been about how women need to change – how they need to change themselves, how they need to change their look, how they need to change their bodies, how they need to change their behaviour, how they need to change their outlook and lean in to work better in business, how they need to . . . OK, we'll stop, we can almost hear you shouting 'All right. We get it. The thing you need to change now is the record.'

But as we look forward, there's now a recognition that it can't all be on women. Men need to change too – and meet women at least halfway. But, to date, men have been pretty much impervious to the gender discussion – and for very interesting reasons. Jack Urwin, who has written one of the conspicuously few books on modern masculinity (it's called *Man Up*, definitely read it, it's very heartfelt and quite funny and bloggy), wrote about this lack of engagement:

> During successive waves of feminism, women have explored different tactical approaches to redefine themselves against an oppression that stretches back beyond recorded history. Men, however, failed. We never had conversations among ourselves about this realignment, and nor did we seek to engage effectively with what was being said around us. Even gay rights activists and feminists struggled to get along. Instead, we doubled down and hoped it might all go away. The cultural thuggery of 90s laddism was business as usual, the same pernicious attitudes allowed to continue, merely disguised with a veneer of irony.[63]

This historical lack of male engagement with the gender redefinition discussion has, inevitably, led to all sorts of problems – for men, for women, in fact for anyone (which is probably almost everyone) who would like to flourish elsewhere on the gender continuum. It means that men are, in every sense of the word, repressing themselves, rigidly sticking to a narrow script of what it means to be a man that has barely changed in fifty years. In the 1970s a sociologist called Robert Brannon laid out four tenets that he described as the basic 'rules' of masculinity in the US. They were 'No Sissy Stuff', which meant avoiding any behaviours or preferences that could be considered feminine, but especially the highly stigmatized feminine behaviours of openness or vulnerability. Concealing or denying emotions was a central part of that definition. Then there was 'The Sturdy Oak', which was defined as 'a manly air of toughness, confidence and self-reliance' that came with expectations to 'be a male machine' – in other words, solve problems without help, maintain emotional self-control at all times and never show weakness to anyone. The third rule was 'The Big Wheel', which was basically the need for status and success: to be looked up to and respected whether that was at work, in sport, or by 'your wife and children' (note, the looking-up bit and where that leads in terms of all the brandsplaining talking-down, diminishing, belittling stuff that we've been discussing). And then there was the fourth characteristic 'Give 'Em Hell', which was all about adventure, taking physical risks, and using violence where necessary.[64]

Five decades later that description of masculinity remains instantly recognizable and barely changed – probably because the very nature of those codes would have prohibited engagement with the limitations contained within them. The journalist Liz Plank, who has recently published a very good book called *For the Love of Men*, describes this idea that the very rules of masculinity actively discourage the questioning of them. In a very good little metaphoric take on the well-worn theme of men and directions, she describes how men are reluctant – as on the road, as in life – to admit that they are lost:

Confessing they are lost is interpreted as an admission of fault. This explains why they will often double down rather than pull over. 'I know the way' he will grumble while she is in the passenger seat rolling her eyes into oblivion . . . The more I read about men's relationship to directions and maps, the more it explained the absence of a substantive and open conversation about masculinity. While women are encouraged to ask questions, men are expected to pretend like they know everything even when they don't, even when it comes to large and existential questions about their gender and their lives.[65]

This disinclination to ask questions or admit confusion explains why the definitions of masculinity are so stubborn and hard to shift – and why, it must therefore follow, so much of the debate ends up being about how women need to change while men must stubbornly double down. There have certainly been trends and fashions in masculinity that have come and gone over the time that we've been working. There was the New Man (remember him and that Athena poster 'Man Holds Baby'?). Then there was all the laddism of *Loaded* etc. Then came the Metrosexual (think how weird that was . . . the idea of a man who showed a slight interest in grooming being so exceptional – and presumably threatening – to the rest of the manly pack, that he had to be cordoned off from the rest and assigned a special name to explain his abnormality). More recently, there's been the Lumbersexual – that almost-pastiche of the log-cutting, wood-carving, rural-dwelling, beard-wearing hipster who mainly lives in Hoxton. And then we had (according to Mark Simpson who originally coined the Metrosexual term) a new variant – the Spornosexual – who's that ripped combination of porn star and sports hero. But, while these variations on the theme come and then go, the blueprint pretty much resists re-examination. And so this hegemonic masculinity is constantly played out and perpetuated in all sorts of environments and settings. It's there in the culture of schools; it's there in the culture of the workplace; it's there in the home and in the roles and labour division within it (sigh); it's there in music; it's there in the culture of sport and physical fitness.

And it has certainly been there – very, very strongly – in the way that marketing has historically treated men and depicted masculinity. From the ruggedness of the Marlboro Man (and his lesser known 'Where a man belongs' Camel-smoking bro) to the sophisticated heroism of the man in the Hathaway shirt; from the top-dog status of 'Gillette: the best a man can get' to the 'spray and play' promise of Axe/Lynx; from the dark and violent world of gaming brands to the endless adventuring 'drive of your life' narratives of the automotive category; from the 'golf-playing smart guy' archetype of many business-to-business presentations to the 'come all challengers' bring your game propositions of the big sports brands; from the 'it's not for girls' machismo of rugged bars of chocolate to the Jack the Lad promises of most early twenty-first-century beer advertising – marketing has a proud tradition (well done you Big Wheels) of standing up these narrow male archetypes.

And we still see it regularly played out in the development of marketing today. Only a few years ago, we went to a meeting to figure out a positioning for a brand where a tool (no, don't rush to that conclusion, we're not using it in the urban dictionary sense) called the NeedScope was being used to explore various benefit territories. It uses the theory of Jungian archetypes, and basically attempts to summarize all the different human needs into useful personas in order that a brand can align its personality and purpose with the needs and personality of its audience.[66] There are (and there's slight variation on this, depending on the different versions of the model) twelve essential archetypes: Innocent, Sage, Explorer, Ruler, Caregiver, Creator, Outlaw, Magician, Hero, Lover, Jester and Everyman. At the meeting, it became obvious nine of the twelve archetypes were assumed by the team working on the project to be male (Caregiver, Innocent and Lover were the only ones ascribed to women; there was a bit of a debate about Creator, but that was put in the male box once it was understood that it was all about innovation), but also that the palette that remained still boxed men into places and cast them in roles that were pretty much identical to Robert Brannon's definitions from the seventies.

And you can see the effect of that embedded thinking in brand after brand and ad after ad. Risk taking is lionized; brooding and emotional distance are promoted; enhanced performance and 'winning' the game are embedded, in some way, into almost all propositions. We recently did a project for a spirits and beer producer and almost every brand in their portfolio played out one of the male stereotypes: the brooding emotionally closed 'Big Wheel' whisky; the daring individualist vodka; the ale that replicated the 'Sturdy Oak' values of self-reliance and toughness; the swashbuckling adventure-chasing rum. And throughout absolutely No Sissy Stuff (unless it was in the form of an admiring lady chasing her hero).

These stereotypes and their stubborn persistence are, in their own way, as punishing as the Good Girl stereotypes that we discussed in Part One. Even men who don't conform to the stereotypes know what they are and often, in some sense, measure themselves, or feel they need to justify themselves, against them. Grayson Perry, who has written and directed and narrated and even potted a lot on this subject, comes up with a brilliant metaphor for a kind of mental watchtower in which most men are captured: 'Men are performing for an invisible authority, the Department of Masculinity. We never know when we are being observed, so we constantly keep watch on ourselves and each other; we guard the boundaries of the role. We are all the authority figure and the prisoner.'[67]

In the last few years, however, there have been some indications that the tight boxes that define masculinity are about to burst open, and that men are engaging more openly in a re-examination of the notions and roles of masculinity. This has partly been driven by men wanting to (or needing to) play, or at least participate in, different roles. In the UK in the 1980s, close to half of men agreed that 'a man's job is to earn money; a woman's job is to look after the home and family'; now only 13 per cent subscribe to that view. Unsurprisingly, beneath this average figure there's an age difference, with only 4 per cent of eighteen- to twenty-five-year-olds agreeing with the statement as opposed to 28 per cent of over sixty-fives.[68] Interestingly, a more traditional picture emerges in the US. In 1994, 42 per cent of male high-school seniors believed the best model was a man working and a woman at home, and the figure has now actually jumped to 58 per cent (grrrr . . . Trump . . . cultural nostalgia . . . grrrr).[69]

But, slowly, and in a two steps forward, one pussy grabbing step back sort of a way, men are gradually pushing for the expansion of their roles. Expectations of fatherhood have changed significantly: in a recent survey conducted by Dove, 85 per cent of fathers in the seven countries surveyed agreed that they 'would do anything' to be more involved with caring after their child was born (two steps forward) but only 33 per cent ended up taking their full allowance of paternity leave (one step back).[70] Some enlightened companies and governments have recognized that giving men their own separate paternity leave on a take-it-or-lose-it basis encourages men to feel able to claim, and not to feel that the leave automatically 'belongs' to the mother. Germany introduced a scheme that allowed dads to receive their own two months' leave and take-up went from 3.3 per cent to 29.3 per cent.[71] A 2019 report by Unicef that analysed legally protected leave for parents in forty-one of the world's richest countries found that twenty-six now offered paid paternity leave, while forty had paid leave for new mothers. The number of countries that offer some form of statutory paternity leave has risen from forty to ninety-four between 1994 and 2015.[72] All excellent two-steps-forward progress. However, it remains the fairly shocking case that in the US (hello again) neither mothers nor fathers are covered by any national paid leave policy. The only available leave, under the Family and Medical Leave Act, is unpaid and covers only around 60 per cent of Americans: very much one step back.

But what is really beginning to change is the understanding of the negative impacts of these narrow boxes on men's health and happiness, and the emerging evidence of their clear harmful effects. Boys are four times more likely than girls to have behavioural, emotional or social difficulties and they are three times as likely to be temporarily excluded from school. Ninety-five per cent of prisoners are male, as are three-quarters of suicides. The author of *Shattered*, Rebecca Asher, who has also written a very insightful book addressing the question of how boys become better men, makes the point that

> whereas the life-long effects of stereotyping on girls are apparent and actively monitored – eating disorders, sexual harassment, domestic inequalities, the motherhood earnings penalty, lack of career progression and so on – the future effect on boys is less well understood. It manifests itself in a lack of close friendships, sexist attitudes towards women and family life, workplace stress, experience of violence and poorer health.[73]

Concerns about the repressing effects of masculinity and their impact on mental health are now more readily discussed, but their widespread prevalence is still undercalled. It's not just the fact that men are encouraged to suppress their emotions, it's the fact that they often feel shame about even having them in the first place. The therapist Terry Real thinks that millions of men are, in fact, living with 'covert depression', which he describes as 'a silent epidemic in men'. Many of the negative behaviours associated with men, such as anger issues, abusive behaviours or alcohol or drug abuse, are often, in fact, attempts to escape mental illness. Workaholism is another. As Grayson Perry describes it, 'often men don't even realize they're sad. Boys are brought up to unconsciously feel they would be breaking their man contract if they were to cry too much. That's why men kill themselves more – they bottle up, bottle up, bottle up, bottle up, until they're overwhelmed by it.'[74]

These harmful definitions of masculinity also make it harder for men to develop and maintain simple relationships: as Liz Plank says, 'if you aren't trained to understand your own emotions, it's fairly predictable that you'll have difficulty understanding the emotions of others. Because men are encouraged to play games that centre on competition rather than relationships, emotional intelli-gence is a muscle that is underdeveloped.'[75] As a result, men have fewer friends and less-deep friendships and become increasingly isolated with age. In the UK alone there are 2.5 million men who report having zero close friends. And the effects of this isolation are profound: as Plank says, 'Loneliness is one of the main predictors for middle-aged white men, the most at risk demographic for tak-ing one's life.'[76]

The slowly building awareness – at a cultural if not yet quite at a personal level – of the crushing effects of 'the man box' on men – and by extension on women – are now emerging into a new set of 'rules' and approaches for marketing that not only are a relaxation and an opening up of the rigid 'for him' / 'for her' delineations of the past, but also often actively seek to challenge and dismantle them. In the new era, pink and blue segregations are dissolved: the conversation about 'the feminine' no longer takes place in isolation from 'the masculine'; the interdependence between 'male' roles and restrictions and 'female' roles and restrictions is acknowledged; the narrative moves from one that's about affirming the 'things that men do' and criticizing 'the things that women are' to a place where men and women work and develop together. In the new era, as the Nigerian author Chimamanda Ngozi Adichie tells us in *We Should All Be Feminists*, a feminist is defined as someone who 'believes in the social, economic and political equality of the sexes'.[77]

No more 'femvertising' targeted just at women

So, the first new approach has to be an end to – or rather an expand-ing of – femvertising where the 'fem' extends to accommodate anyone 'who believes in the social, economic and political equality of the sexes'. We've discussed how a fatal flaw of the femvertising era was the focus on cheerleading women to change themselves: the 'fix the women' narratives that spoke only to women and were, very often, encouraging them to become more like men. And how, despite its apparently benign approaches, it was often a wolf in sheep's clothing, silkily telling women that something was wrong with what they were. As a result, however gently or smoothly or cheeringly, the intention was to regulate and discipline their behaviour: to put it on women while leaving men's role in the piece unexamined.

In the new era, there needs to be a recognition that these approaches are incomplete, reflect only one half of the problem and, as usual, leave women to do the work (sigh again). The conversation now needs to include men and, instead of just telling women how they need to change to be 'up' to men, suggest to men how they might need to change to meet women halfway. *GQ* recently did a whole issue on 'New Masculinity' (it got a lot of flak and pushback, as you can imagine), and it contained this advice from the Australian comedian Hannah Gadsby:

Hello, the men. My advice on modern masculinity would be to look at all those traits you believe are feminine and interrogate why you are so obsessed with being the opposite. Because this idea that to be a man you have to be the furthest away from being a woman that you possibly can is really weird.

Why is everyone so scared of not being masculine? If you consider many of those in power, those who claim to be 'leading' the world at the moment, you've got a lot of hypermasculine man-babies, with terrible hair and no ability to compromise. These are the cool guys who are taking us all to hell in a handbasket they didn't pay for.

So here's a thought experiment: What if you, the men, looked to traditional feminine traits and tried incorporating them into your masculinity?

Women are always being encouraged to stir masculine traits into their feminine recipe. We are told to 'be bolder!' 'Speak up in meetings.' 'Exaggerate your skills.' All that *Lean In* sort of crap. So perhaps it's time for you, the men, to be more ladylike. How about you scale back on your confidence? How about you try not to act in every situation? What if you tried to refrain from sharing your opinions or co-opting other people's ideas? How about yielding to people walking in the opposite direction? Or even just attempting to see them?[78]

There have been a very few efforts made by marketing to invite men in – and encourage them to develop (to use the old partisan language) their 'feminine side'. In 2017, the makers of American Girl announced their very first male doll: a perfect looking boy-band type wearing a blue lumberjack shirt (obvs) over a Play Loud T-shirt (obvs again – it would have been too much to hope for a T-shirt saying Play Nicely). His name was Logan Everett and he was a massive hit. He was such a hit, in fact, that in one piece of promo material, he was shown centre stage 'holding and singing into the mic' while a blonde, blank-looking American Girl hovered in the background, singing backing and looking admiringly on (obvs, obvs, obvs and obvs again). But Logan also produced some horrible backlash of the Jordan Peterson 'Let Boys Be Boys' school.[79] And a sad Pew survey amongst men showed that while 72 per cent agreed that girls should be encouraged to play with toys traditionally designed for boys, only 56 per cent felt comfortable with boys playing with girls' toys.[80]

In the parenting space, there's been a bit of development too. There are now quite a few brands of changing bags designed for men – but it's conspicuous how, just like Logan Everett, they conform to very traditional male archetypes. Most of them are monochrome (aka serious), most of them are made to look like backpacks (aka rugged) or briefcases (aka business Big Wheel), most of them have those tool-belt loops and outer pockets that you get on military or outdoor gear (aka strong and industrial). There's even a brand called, wait for it, Tactical Baby Gear that basically treats the task of looking after a baby as military combat: the bags are made from camo fabric, they have names like the MOD Panel 002 (no kidding), and, while there's obviously some claim to irony going on, there's a completely unreconstructed hero and protector narrative playing out. Here's how they describe their – in big black capital letters – **BULLET PROOF PANELS**:

> At Tactical Baby Gear®, we hope your family never faces a crisis more severe than a full diaper on a long road trip. But we also recognize the dangers families face in this day and age, which is why every one of our diaper bags and backpacks have been designed since day one to accommodate body armor and help you keep your loved ones safe.[81]

In male beauty, there's often a similar thing going on. Packaging tends to the black and the bold, with lots of go-fast stripes to indicate power and performance. And there's an equivalent of the Tactical Baby Gear approach here too: a brand called War Paint that got into lots of trouble last year for a launch communication that featured a tattooed white man, flexing his pecs, using the products and then putting on a big skull ring. This, it seemed to be saying, is the brand for real men (subtext: not like all those other lightweight loser brands for [insert 'No Sissy Stuff' name-calling here]). Again, it induced a massive Twitter pile-on of accusations that the brand was actually using toxic masculinity to sell make-up: 'the sort of men who like make-up aren't the Axe body spray circa 2000s type; hope to see your comms explore other flavours of masculinity'.

It's possible to see what these sorts of efforts are trying to do – and, in the spirit of meeting halfway, their hearts are in the right place. But, in reality, they're as insulting and restrictive as the pink phones and pens and drills and guns and cars of the twentieth century – embedding stereotypes even as they try to break out of them.

Challenge traditional masculinity

In the new era, brands need to encourage new and extended and positive definitions of masculinity and get over their base-setting habits of sticking to the old tropes and boxes that reduce both men and women. No more unreconstructed Big Wheel, or Sturdy Oak or Give 'Em Hell or No Sissy Stuff, but a more open, expanded (Star Burst New Improved) version that presents men as sensitive, thoughtful, concerned for others, complex, loving.

If, as a brand, you feel you need a place to start you could do a lot worse than home in on these 'rules' (actually they're – appropriately – more gentle guidelines) of non-traditional masculinity that were produced by Grayson Perry:[82]

1. **Open up**

   'Being vulnerable is the absolute key to having good relationships. And good relationships are the key to being happy.'

2. **Bravado comes in many forms**

   'Men are very good at bungee jumping or driving fast, things that are physically dangerous, but they're not so good at emotional bravery, such as having that difficult conversation with a colleague or partner. Men often cringe; they can't handle it. I'm probably better than most because, having been through many embarrassing situations, I've learned that you don't die.'

3. **Don't get too hung up on identity issues**

   'The idea of gender fluidity is an alien concept to the vast majority of people, even in Britain.'

4. **Look to the future**

   'Men are always looking back to a time when men were men and trying to bring that back. I'm saying you've got to look forward, mate. Women are always looking forward. Feminism always looks to how women can be – and that's fine. It doesn't stop them being women.'

5. **Embrace your costume**

   'All men wear costumes – they just don't think of it as a costume. That's the thing about masculinity; it sees itself as this sort of default position, so therefore everything else

is dressing up, whereas the man is just being normal. Men
might not have frills and furbelows as women
traditionally do, but they've got spurious function: knobs
on their watches or extra pockets on their jackets that are
just as decorative as anything women wear.'

6. Channel your painful past into useful things

'We all find ways to comfort ourselves, or reinterpret
experiences to make them seem OK. For me it was art; for
other people it can be sport.'

7. Feminism is your friend

'Men need not be scared of it. But the name puts them
off – it has 'feminine' in it. I don't think enough is talked
about the rewards for men from gender equality. Women
have clear goals to gain from it that are easy to measure –
such as pay – whereas men stand to gain emotional
benefits and become happier, which is harder to measure.'

8. Realise there's a problem

'It's difficult convincing men that there's a problem with
masculinity because they are the least equipped people to
realise they are lacking things on an emotional level.'

9. Change can be subtle

'Men need to learn how nice it is to be nice, how to be
more empathetic to the world. It's a simple, sloshy thing to
say, but lots of men are hooked into proving that they are
men too much. It's to their own detriment, as much as
everyone else's. I want them to be happier, that's all.'

10. Taking risks is part of our nature

'Men are predisposed to taking risks, and that's fine – I
love risks: get me on a mountain bike or a motor bike, I
love it. I'm an adrenaline addict. It's the same with public
speaking or becoming a part of a public conversation –
these are all risky strategies that can go terribly wrong.'

11. Let your children be themselves

'Parents in this country often know their child's gender
before they are born, so they start the gendering process

on the foetus. They're already talking to it in their stomach and getting their mindset on how they will treat their child.'

12. Think about how macho pursuits affect the world
'Just look at Isis and what it promises to those young boys who go to fight. You're in a group, there's a clear goal – it's a real masculine adventure. There's not much negotiation going on!'

Gillette's 'Best a Man Can Be' 2019 advertising was a brave attempt to go down the route of challenging traditional masculinity and examining its negative impacts. Predictably perhaps the ad triggered an immense amount of backlash – as well as praise for opening a discourse that examined how men might need to change, not just how women needed to fix themselves. Beyond the normal old conservative voices, much of the backlash against the campaign seemed to be driven by accusations of hypocrisy and bandwagon-jumping – how could a brand that for decades had stood up the competitive 'best a man can get' hierarchical view of masculinity as a game to be won now suddenly question the consequences? But that observation actually misses the point. In fact, it almost is the point: questioning and being unafraid of change is not a mark of hypocrisy but a sign of enlightenment. The ad was, in that sense, an example of itself.

Axe has also had a bit of a Damascene moment with their 'Is It OK for Guys To . . .' campaign that questions head-on the limitations and restrictions of the masculine archetypes and promotes the idea of 'being yourself'. It presumably got a bit of flak too, but never mind – as with Gillette, when the 'Big Boys' (see how pervasive it is) of the male-brand world turn good, it's better for everyone.

And it's infectious – as with Dove and the first forays into fem-powerment: once one does it, all the walls come tumbling down. As a case in point Harry's – the new kid on the shaving block – followed Gillette's foray with an interesting and actually rather moving short film – *A Man Like You*. As a newer brand with less baggage, it's perhaps easier for them to explore the space, but it's beautifully done and also pulls off the trick of including women in the conversation. Look it up if you haven't seen it.[83] (As a quite funny aside, when it was launched the founder of Harry's, Andy Katz-Mayfield, took to Twitter to explain how their version of masculinity was basically better than Gillette's (and therefore presumably the best a man can actually be): 'the way that we view masculinity is a little more expansive and nuanced and complicated [than Gillette's]. This video was an attempt to start a conversation around that.' What did we say about the old, competitive, self-reinforcing habits of masculinity and how they die hard?)

Sins of your fathers

As category and gender lines continue to blur, and audiences and brands continue to jump the ropes, there's a need to learn from the negative impacts of what has gone before and to avoid simply following an on-a-loop repeat of how things have been done historically. We talked a lot in Part One about how the slow, slow drip of beauty communications had contributed to the growth in prevalence of eating disorders in women, and we are now seeing many of those same horrible effects when it comes to men. In men, body dysmorphia typically takes the form of muscle dysmorphia – sometimes called bigorexia: a preoccupation that the body is too small or puny, which results in a disordered concern with muscle building, overtraining with weights and overuse of protein supplements. It's a horrible obverse of the eating disorders in girls and women: where in women, the drive is to go smaller, slighter, less, in men it is to become big, stronger, more. And like so many of the inflictions impacting on men, it is a silent epidemic: a study published in June 2019 found that 22 per cent of men in the US aged eighteen to twenty-four reported muscularity-oriented disordered eating, and another estimated that 10 per cent of men in UK gyms were suffering but didn't acknowledge their problem to themselves, let alone the world.[84] In addition, the number of adult men being admitted to hospital with an eating disorder has risen by 70 per cent over the past six years. During these years, the male beauty and grooming industry has grown and grown: barber shops are popping up at exponential rates; new brands are launching almost every week. Given what is now known about the harmful effects of marketing on women's self-perception, are some of the sins of the fathers now being replayed to a whole new audience of impressionable and vulnerable young men?

Conclusion: From Master to Patron and now to Servant

So, there they are – ten principles that we believe describe a new conversation between brands and their female audiences and a new vision for marketing to women to take us into the next and the new era.

When we look back at where we set off – both with this book and with our business – the world of marketing to women was determined by a relationship where the masculine brand assumed an immediate and higher authority over the audience; where (and now we're at the end we'll just remind you of some of Rebecca Solnit's words with which we began) it treats the female audience as 'an empty vessel to be filled with their wisdom and knowledge'; where the brand tells women what they are and what they can be; where the brand is so busy 'holding forth, eyes fixed on the fuzzy far horizon of its own authority' that it fails to properly listen to or even really see the audience; the audience – in their 'assigned role as ingénue' – is left feeling reduced, doubtful and secondary; and all this happens in a way that is 'usually so sneaky and hard to point out' that challenging it feels difficult or unreasonable (and thus the issue and the unhealthy relationship continue unchecked as 'par for the course').

And we've shown – in our journey from 'how we got here' to 'where we are now' – how that 'splaining relationship changed: in surface ways apparently boldly, but in deeper and more fundamental ways not at all. We described how brands moved from behaving like obvious masters in their field to becoming patrons of women, adopting a moral authority, saving women from themselves or the beastly sexist ways in which the brand or the category had behaved in the past. The brandsplaining continued, but in new, more disguised and in some cases more pernicious ways.

But that relationship – either in its obvious master form or as the more covert patron – now has to end. Women – as we've shown – are not there waiting, listening quietly, ready to 'be told': they're out there, getting their voices heard, calling out the stuff that's wrong and – across almost every life stage, every demographic group, every market and every part of popular culture – making their presence strong and strongly felt. And as consumers, they're not sitting nicely either: in fact, they're using every tool in the digital box to find exactly what they want on the terms that they want it.

To succeed in this new context, brands need – to put it bluntly – to get down from on high and back in their box. No more assuming a higher authority. No more telling women how and why they're wrong. No more telling women that they need to change. Instead, brands need to get down, get busy and make themselves useful. They need to earn respect and prove their worth. In short, it is time to manage brands as if they exist to serve women. Master and patron are no longer sustainable positions: instead, in the new era, the brand needs to see itself as a servant, working for women and solving the things that they want solved. Our hope is that this book – and the ten principles that we've described – will allow that new relationship to form and to flourish, for the greater health and happiness of both female consumers and the brands that should always have been in the business of serving them.

Notes

Part One: How We Got Here

1 Rachel Simmons, *The Curse of the Good Girl: Raising Authentic Girls with Courage and Confidence* (New York: Penguin, 2009).

2 Office for National Statistics (ONS) Annual Survey of Hours and Earnings (ASHE) 2019; www.ons.gov.uk/releases/employeeearnings intheuk2019.

3 Laura Mulvey, 'Visual Pleasure and Narrative Cinema', *Screen*, Autumn 1975.

4 Marlen Komar, 'L'Oreal's "Because You're Worth It" Origin Story is Feminist as Hell', *Bustle*, 19 November 2017; www.bustle.com/p/loreals-because-youre-worth-it-origin-story-is-feminist-as-hell-73630.

5 Michael J. Silverstein and Kate Sayre, 'The Female Economy', *Harvard Business Review*, September 2009.

6 Fara Warner, *The Power of the Purse: How Smart Businesses are Adapting to the World's Most Important Consumers – Women* (New York: Pearson, 2005); she-conomy.com (Stephanie Holland's 'A guy's guide to marketing to women' website).

7 www.campaignlive.co.uk/article/stop-press-equal-opportunities-commission-launches-new-logo/77288.

8 Julia Serano, *Whipping Girl: A Transsexual Woman on Sexism and the Scapegoating of Femininity* (New York: Seal Press, 2007).

9 Jane Cunningham and Philippa Roberts, *Inside Her Pretty Little Head: A New Theory of Female Motivation and What It Means for Marketing* (London: Cyan Books, 2006).

10 Liz Plank, *For the Love of Men: A New Vision for Mindful Masculinity* (New York: St Martin's Press, 2019).

11 Helga Dittmar and Sarah Howard, 'Thin-Ideal Internalization and Social Comparison Tendency as Moderators of Media Models' Impact

on Women's Body-Focused Anxiety', *Journal of Social and Clinical Psychology*, 23(6) (2004).

12 Tom Reichert and Courtney Carpenter, 'An Update on Sex in Magazine Advertising 1983 to 2003', *Journalism & Mass Communication Quarterly*, December 2004.

13 Adrian Furnham and Stephanie Paltzer, 'The Portrayal of Men and Women in Television Advertisements: An Updated Review of 30 Studies Published Since 2000', *Scandinavian Journal of Psychology*, 51(3) (2010).

14 Tom Reichert, Courtney Carpenter Childers and Leonard N. Reid, 'How Sex in Advertising Varies by Product Category: An Analysis of Three Decades of Visual Sexual Imagery in Magazine Advertising', *Journal of Current Issues & Research in Advertising*, 33(1) (2012).

Part Two: Where We Are Now

1 Katty Kay and Claire Shipman, *The Confidence Code for Girls: Taking Risks, Messing Up and Becoming Your Amazingly Imperfect, Totally Powerful Self* (New York: HarperCollins, 2018).

2 Girls' Attitudes Survey. Girl Guiding and Childwise. Report (2012); www.girlguiding.org.uk/girls-making-change/girls-attitudes-survey/.

3 Claire Howorth, 'The Goddess Myth', *Time* magazine, October 2017; https://time.com/4989068/motherhood-is-hard-to-get-wrong/.

4 'Stress: Are We Coping?' Mental Health Foundation, UK, May 2018 survey; www.mentalhealth.org.uk/news/stressed-nation-74-uk-over whelmed-or-unable-cope-some-point-past-year.

5 NHS Digital, Hospital admissions for eating disorders, October 2019.

6 In partnership with Mindshare London, a global media and marketing services company, we (PLH) conducted a study in 2019 that investigated attitudes to marketing and female identity amongst a sample of 14,000 women of all backgrounds, lifestyles and ages and across five continents. The intention in the study was to help us understand whether the state of marketing to women as suggested by our content analysis is aligned with where women feel it should be,

and whether or not it aligns with how women see themselves (hereafter PLH/Mindshare study (2019)).

7 Ibid.

8 Ibid.

9 'Share of Weibo Users Among China's Online Population 2010–2018'; www.statista.com/statistics/739702/china-share-of-weibo-users/.

10 'TikTok User Ratio in the US 2020 by Gender'; www.statista.com/statistics/1095201/tiktok-users-gender-usa.

11 Women's Sport: 'Say Yes to Success' (2014 report); www.womeninsport.org/wp-content/uploads/2015/04/Media-Stats-Pack-June-2015.pdf.

12 'Women's World Cup Soccer Final Scores New Twitter Record With 7,196 Tweets Per Second'; https://techcrunch.com/2011/07/17/womens-world-cup-soccer-final-scores-new-twitter-record-with-7196-tweets-per-second.

13 Real time subscriber stats for YouTube, at time of writing, from https://socialblade.com.

14 'Distribution of NFL Television Audience During Regular Season by Race/Ethnicity', www.statista.com/statistics/289952/distribution-of-nfl-regular-season-tv-audience-by-race-or-ethnicity/.

15 Rebecca Traister, *Good and Mad: The Revolutionary Power of Women's Anger* (New York: Simon & Schuster, 2018).

16 Study by Women in Journalism between 5 June and 22 July 2017 of front-page stories in UK national newspapers; womeninjournalism.co.uk. 'The Status of Women in the U.S. Media 2019', a report published by the Women's Media Center, found that 63 per cent of by-lines in US national newspapers are male.

17 The Fawcett Society, 'Sex and Power 2020'; www.fawcettsociety.org.uk/sex-and-power-2020.

18 Global Media Monitoring Project, 'Who Makes the News?' (2015); http://whomakesthenews.org/gmmp/gmmp-reports/gmmp-2015-reports.

19 4th Estate, 'Silenced: Gender Gap in the 2012 US Election Coverage, Studying a Total of 2750 Print Articles and TV Segments in the Six-Month Period from November 1st to May 15th'.

20 Martha M. Lauzen, 'The Celluloid Ceiling. Behind-the-Scenes Employment of Women on the Top 100, 250 and 500 films of 2018',

Center for the Study of Women in Television and Film, https://
womenintvfilm.sdsu.edu/wp-content/uploads/2020/01/2019_Celluloid_
Ceiling_Report.pdf.

21 'Diversity and Inclusivity Report: Gender in YouTube Advertising 2019',
https://seejane.org/research-informs-empowers/diversity-inclusivity-
report-gender-in-youtube-advertising/.

22 Nathalie Remy, Eveline Speelman and Steven Swartz, 'Style That's
Sustainable: A New Fast-Fashion Formula', McKinsey and Company, 20
October 2016; www.mckinsey.com/business-functions/sustainability/
our-insights/style-thats-sustainable-a-new-fast-fashion-formula.

23 Lyst Insights, 'The 2020 Conscious Fashion Report'; An analysis of the
last 12 months from February 2019 to February 2020 of searches for
fashion products on Lyst. Searches include looking at the 100 million
shoppers using the platform, Google search data, active browsing
page views and conversion rates and sales; www.lyst.com/data/2020-
conscious-fashion-report/.

24 Fashion Revolution, self-reporting annual data 2020.

25 Ibid.

26 Avivah Wittenberg-Cox and Alison Maitland, *Why Women Mean Business* (Chichester: Wiley, 2008); Avivah Wittenberg-Cox. *How Women Mean Business* (Chichester: Wiley, 2010).

27 US CMOs: Forbes, Russell Reynolds Associates, 2019 data based on
an analysis of more than 200 senior marketing job changes during the
first half of the year. UK CMOs: AXONN 2018; 45 per cent female
CMOs, derived from online survey run in January 2017 and responses
from those who have some sort of marketing responsibility in their
organization.

28 According to Glassdoor recruitment, the average salary for executive
creative director in 2020 was in the region of £135,000; www.glassdoor.
co.uk/.

29 Lili Loofbourow, 'The Male Glance', *Virginia Quarterly Review*, 5
March 2018; www.vqronline.org/essays-articles/2018/03/male-glance.

30 Ibid.

31 PLH/Mindshare study (2019).

32 PLH content analysis method: Sample 120 of the biggest spending brands on TV, in categories that traditionally target women: apparel, household products, feminine hygiene, health and beauty (to include haircare, skincare, make-up), luxury branded products, retail and babycare. In addition to those categories we have also interrogated sixty-five ads in markets which either usually target men or target a mix of men and women: cars, insurance, banking and telecoms. We also analysed the websites and packaging of eighty brands, in feminine hygiene, health and beauty (to include haircare, skincare, make-up) and household products. Social media is, of course, a channel that brands are using more and more as a way of connecting with their customers, so we have also analysed the Instagram feeds and where relevant the YouTube channels of the brands we used in the TV analysis. In addition, we looked at a sample of advertising and brands which specifically target men (e.g. in skincare and haircare), to benchmark our thinking and to make comparisons.

33 https://seejane.org/.

34 Ibid.

35 PLH/Mindshare study (2019).

36 Dittmar and Howard, 'Thin-Ideal Internalization'.

37 PLH/Mindshare study (2019).

38 Ibid.

39 PLH content analysis, see note 32.

40 Alyssa Saiphoo and Zahra Vahedi, 'A Meta-Analytic Review of the Relationship Between Social Media Use and Body Image Disturbance', *Computers in Human Behavior*, July 2019; https://doi.org/10.1016/j.chb.2019.07.028.

41 PLH content analysis, see note 32.

42 Ibid.

43 Barra Roantree and Kartik Vira, 'The Rise and Rise of Women's Employment in the UK', Institute for Fiscal Studies, 2018; www.ifs.org.uk/uploads/BN234.pdf.

44 *Wall Street Journal*, 10 January 2020, citing Bureau of Labor statistics from December 2019.

45 PLH content analysis, see note 32.

46 ONS, Overview of the UK population: August 2019; www.ons. gov.uk/peoplepopulationandcommunity/populationandmigration/ populationestimates/articles/overviewoftheukpopulation/august2019.

47 YouGov Channel 4 study of 1,000 advertisements shown in the UK in two months of 2019.

48 PLH/Mindshare study (2019).

49 Of the sample in the PLH/Mindshare study 55 per cent say there is not enough diversity in advertising.

50 www.thedrum.com/news/2020/01/27/olay-s-super-bowl-return-unapologetically-female-we-re-changing-the-narrative.

51 Loofbourow, 'The Male Glance'.

52 Helen Lewis, *Difficult Women: A History of Feminism in 11 Fights* (New York: Vintage, 2020).

53 Ibid.

Part Three: Where We Go Next

1 Department for Education (DfE) National Curriculum Assessments, Key Stage 2, 2019; www.gov.uk/government/organisations/department-for-education.

2 Joint Council for Qualifications (JCQ) 2019; jcq.org.uk.

3 Ibid.

4 Ibid.

5 *Guardian*, 15 August 2019. Female students outnumber males in A-level science entries. Data from Joint Council for Qualifications. Base: combined number of chemistry, physics and biology A levels sat in England 2019.

6 Rachel Hewitt, 'Mind the Gap: Gender Differences in Higher Education', Higher Education Policy Institute, March 2020; www.hepi.ac. uk/2020/03/07/mind-the-gap-gender-differences-in-higher-education/.

7 Stéphan Vincent-Lancrin for the OECD Centre for Educational Research and Innovation (CERI), 'The Reversal of Gender Inequalities in Higher Education: An On-going Trend', chapter 10 in *Higher Education*

to 2030, vol. 1: *Demography* (OECD 2008); www.oecd.org/education/ceri/41939699.pdf.

8 Rebecca Traister, *All the Single Ladies: Unmarried Women and the Rise of an Independent Nation* (New York: Simon & Schuster, 2016).

9 ONS, Marriages in England and Wales; www.ons.gov.uk/peoplepopula tionandcommunity/birthsdeathsandmarriages/marriagecohabitation andcivilpartnerships/bulletins/marriagesinenglandandwalesprovis ional/2017.

10 'Mean Age at First Marriage in Selected European Countries in 2018 by Country and by Gender'; www.statista.com/statistics/612174/mean-age-at-first-marriage-in-european-countries/.

11 Pewsocialtrends.org, December 2014; www.pewsocialtrends.org/2011/12/14/barely-half-of-u-s-adults-are-married-a-record-low/.

12 ONS, Marriages in England and Wales.

13 The *Japan Times* reporting on a study conducted by the National Institute of Population and Social Security Research, 16 September 2016; www.japantimes.co.jp/news/2016/09/16/national/social-issues/sexless-japan-almost-half-young-men-women-virgins-survey/.

14 '33% Of Japanese People Think Marriage Is Pointless', *Japan Today* Survey, July 2013; https://japantoday.com/category/national/33-of-japanese-think-marriage-is-pointless-survey.

15 Eurostat, Marriage and Divorce Statistics 2018; https://ec.europa.eu/eurostat/web/products-eurostat-news/.

16 www.statista.com/statistics/294594/mother-average-age-at-childbirth-england-and-wales-by-child-number/.

17 Brady Hamilton, National Health Statistics, 2018, Centers for Disease Control and Prevention, Report 007, May 2019.

18 PLH/Mindshare study (2019).

19 Ibid.

20 Survey conducted by Megan Dalla-Camina, author of *Getting Real About Having It All: Be Your Best, Love Your Career and Bring Back Your Sparkle*. (Brighton-Le-Sands NSW: Hay House, 2012).

21 'Michelle Obama on Sheryl Sandberg's Lean In Philosophy: "That shit doesn't work all the time!", *Vox*, 3 December 2018; www.vox.com/culture/2018/12/3/18123796/michelle-obama-criticizes-lean-in-becoming-tour.

22 ONS, 'Women Shoulder the Responsibility of "Unpaid Work" '; www. ons.gov.uk/employmentandlabourmarket/peopleinwork/earningsand workinghours/articles/womenshouldertheresponsibilityofunpaidwork/ 2016-11-10.

23 Sally Howard, *The Home Stretch: Why the Gender Revolution Stalled at the Kitchen Sink* (London: Atlantic Books, 2020).

24 Ibid.

25 Christopher Rauh, 'Women Bear Brunt of Coronavirus Economic Shutdown in UK and US', University of Cambridge Institute for New Economic Thinking, April 2020; www.inet.econ.cam.ac.uk/working-paper-pdfs/wp2018.pdf; quote from interview in the *Observer* by Donna Ferguson, 3 May 2020: 'I Feel Like a 1950s Housewife: How Lockdown Has Exposed the Gender Divide'.

26 Eve Rodsky, *Fair Play: Share the Mental Load, Rebalance Your Relationship and Transform Your Life* (London: Quercus, 2019); quote from interview in *Grazia* with Karen Yossman, 18 December 2019.

27 Sally Howard, *The Home Stretch: Why It's Time to Come Clean About Who Does the Dishes* (London: Atlantic Books, 2020).

28 https://oldestvocation.com/2015/05/11/the-silent-generation-and-the-boomers/.

29 *Time*, 6 January 1967; see https://time.com/4607270/1967-january-6-anniversary/.

30 'The Grey Market', *The Economist*, 7 April 2016; www.economist.com/business/2016/04/07/the-grey-market.

31 Andrew Scott and Lynda Gratton, *The New Long Life: A Framework for Flourishing in a Changing World* (London: Bloomsbury, 2020).

32 Halima Khan, '5 Hours a Day: Systemic Innovation for an Ageing Population', Nesta UK Innovation Foundation, February 2013.

33 'Older People Projected to Outnumber Children for First Time in US History', United States Census Bureau, 13 March 2018, Release Number CB18-41; www.census.gov/newsroom/press-releases/2018/cb18-41-population-projections.html.

34 Carl Emmerson, Katherine Heald and Andrew Hood, 'The Changing Face of Retirement', Institute of Fiscal Studies Report R95, June 2014.

35 Mary Portas, 'Future of Retail 2019'; www.raconteur.net/future-retail-2019-dec.

36 Michelle P. King, *The Fix: Overcome the Invisible Barriers That Are Holding Women Back at Work* (New York: Atria Books, 2020).

37 Jennifer L. Berdahl, Peter Glick and Marianne Cooper, 'How Masculinity Contests Undermine Organizations and What To Do About It', *Harvard Business Review*, November 2018.

38 Anne Boden, *Banking On It: How I Disrupted an Industry* (London: Penguin Business, 2020).

39 'Women Will Buy Their Own Damn Jewelry, Thank You Very Much', *Glamour*, 15 November 2019; www.glamour.com/story/women-will-buy-their-own-damn-jewelry.

40 *Telegraph*, 23 May 2015; www.telegraph.co.uk/women/womens-busi ness/11616130/Tinder-co-founder-Whitney-Wolfe-The-word-feminist-seemed-to-put-guys-off-but-now-I-realise-who-cares.html.

41 https://thebeehive.bumble.com/whitneyftob.

42 www.verywellfamily.com/top-mom-blogs-4583002.

43 'The Boss: Jill Smokler Turned Her Parenting Struggles into a Successful Media Company', *Time*, 9 November 2017; https://time.com/5013615/scary-mommy-jill-smokler-the-boss/.

44 'Why Inspiring Women Over 60 Are the Season's Front Row MVPs', *Vogue*, 25 February 2020; www.vogue.com/slideshow/fall-winter-2020-front-row-mvps-stylish-women-over-sixty.

45 PLH/Mindshare study (2019).

46 Lidewij Edelkoort, 'Anti-Fashion: A Manifesto for the Next Decade', published by Trend Union, 2015; www.edelkoort.com.

47 PLH/Mindshare study (2019).

48 www.thirdlove.com/pages/ourstory.

49 *New York Times*, 20 November 2018.

50 *Independent*, 22 May 2019; www.independent.co.uk/life-style/fashion/universal-standard-inclusive-us-fashion-sizes-00-40-clothing-plus-size-a8924781.html.

51 www.universalstandard.com/pages/about-us.

52 https://knix.com/pages/about-us; www.dearkates.com/pages/about-us; www.rubylove.com/about.

53 https://theordinary.deciem.com/about.

54 www.harpersbazaar.com/uk/beauty/make-up-nails/a29576115/milk-makeup/.

55 www.milkmakeup.com, ingredients blacklist.

56 'How Two Dermatologists Built a Billion Dollar Brand in Their Spare Time', *Forbes*, 21 June 2016; www.forbes.com/sites/katevinton/2016/06/01/billion-dollar-brand-proactiv-rodan-fields/#7389594e3bfe.

57 www.academy.makeupforever.com; @dany_sanz_d on Instagram.

58 https://ca.morphe.com/pages/about-morphe.

59 agender.co.kr.

60 www.youtube.com/watch?v=nFUvLNL7E8Q.

61 *Independent*, 23 January 2019; www.independent.co.uk/life-style/fashion/hm-eytys-gender-neutral-unisex-collection-release-lookbook-fashion-a8741996.html.

62 John Berger, *Ways of Seeing* (Harmondsworth: Penguin, 1972).

63 Jack Urwin, *Man Up: Surviving Modern Masculinity* (London: Icon Books, 2016).

64 Robert Brannon, 'The Male Sex Role: Our Culture's Blueprint of Manhood, and What It's Done for Us Lately', in D. David and R. Brannon (eds.), *The Forty-Nine Percent Majority: The Male Sex Role* (Reading, MA: Addison-Wesley, 1976).

65 Liz Plank, *For the Love of Men: From Toxic to a More Mindful Masculinity* (New York: St Martin's Press, 2019).

66 www.needscopeinternational.com/.

67 Grayson Perry, *The Descent of Man* (London: Allen Lane, 2016).

68 PLH/Mindshare study (2019).

69 Council on Contemporary Families study of attitudes amongst high school leavers in the US to gender roles in the family; data compared is 1994 to 2014.

70 Nikki van der Gaag et al., 'State of the World's Fathers: Unlocking the Power of Men's Care'; https://promundoglobal.org/resources/state-of-the-worlds-fathers-unlocking-the-power-of-mens-care/#.

71 The Helping Dads Care Research Project; Promundo and Dove Men+Care 2017–2019; https://promundoglobal.org/resources/helping-dads-care/.

72 Unicef, 'Are the World's Richest Countries Family Friendly? Policy in the OECD and EU', June 2019; www.unicef-irc.org/family-friendly.

73 Rebecca Asher, *Shattered: Modern Motherhood and the Illusion of Equality* (London: Vintage, 2012).

74 Perry, *Descent of Man*; ONS suicides in the UK: 2018 registrations.

75 Plank, *For the Love of Men*.

76 Ibid.

77 Chimamanda Ngozi Adichie, *We Should All Be Feminists* (London: HarperCollins, 2014).

78 'Hannah Gadsby on Why Men Should Be More Ladylike', *GQ* (New Masculinity issue), 15 October 2019; www.gq.com/story/hannah-gadsby-why-men-should-be-more-ladylike.

79 'It's Right and Necessary to Let Boys Be Boys', *National Review*, 27 March 2018; www.nationalreview.com/2018/03/its-right-and-necessary-to-let-boys-be-boys/.

80 Pew Research Center, August and September 2017; www.pewresearch.org/facttank/2017.

81 https://tacticalbabygear.com/collections/bullet-proof-panel.

82 'Grayson Perry's 12 Steps to Becoming a Modern Man', *Guardian*, 4 May 2016; www.theguardian.com/artanddesign/2016/may/04/grayson-perry-all-man-boys-breaking-man-contract-if-they-cry.

83 www.youtube.com/watch?v=jIDLa5zhO8A.

84 Jason M. Nagata et al., 'Predictors of Muscularity-Oriented Disordered Eating Behaviors in U.S. Young Adults: A Prospective Cohort Study', *International Journal of Eating Disorders*, 52(12) (2019); https://doi.org/10.1002/eat.23094. Body Dysmorphic Disorder Foundation UK, 2015; www.bddfoundation.org.

Acknowledgements

We're very grateful for the support, patience and contributions of Matt Willifer, Philip Roberts, William Griffin, Vicky Cook, Susannah Lear, Flora Fraser, Andrew Fraser, Rebecca Wynberg, Patrick Willifer, Maggie Willifer, Rose Roberts, Claire Conrad, Malcolm White, Ian Forth, Anna Hopwood, Nadina Dalea and Jane Sassienie. Thanks too to the many women who authored the studies and books we reference in the text, not least of course to Rebecca Solnit. And final thanks go to 'Steve', for being the catalyst and the fall-guy.

Index